knitting and tea

Published in the United States by Potter Craft,
an imprint of the Crown Publishing Group,
a division of Random House, Inc., New York.
www.crownpublishing.com
www.pottercraft.com

POTTER CRAFT and colophon is a registered
trademark of Random House, Inc.

Library of Congress Cataloging-in-Publication
Data is available upon request.
ISBN 978-0-307-35221-7
Printed in China

Design by Chi Ling Moy

10 9 8 7 6 5 4 3 2 1

First Edition

The author and publisher would like to thank the
Craft Yarn Council of America for providing the
yarn weight standards and accompanying icons
used in this book. For more information, please
visit www.YarnStandards.com.

dedication

To Sarah, my sister and fellow tearoom connoisseur.
Also, to the wonderful people of Sri Lanka, who were so
special to Patrick in his childhood and whose warmth
and hospitality continue to inspire us.

KNITTING AND TEA

25 Classic Knits and the Teas that Inspired Them

Jane Gottelier

photography by **Patrick Gottelier**

POTTER
CRAFT

New York

CONTENTS

INTRODUCTION

There is a lot of speculation surrounding the discovery of knitting—both the date and the location are in dispute among textile historians. However, it is becoming increasingly accepted that knitting as we know it probably started in the Middle East, most likely in Egypt in the eleventh century CE, later spreading to Europe through Moorish Spain. Archaeologists have even unearthed fourteenth-century socks with blessings and prayers knitted into them in Arabic script.

The dating of tea, on the other hand, is more straightforward, but it does rely on a myth. The legend goes that the discovery of tea occurred in ancient China when the Emperor ShenNung in 2737 BCE noticed some leaves had accidentally blown from a tea bush into some boiling water that had been prepared for him to drink. The emperor so liked the delicate flavor that enhanced his drinking water that the art of tea making began and flourished.

But what of knitting and tea—what is the connection? Perhaps the key is that they both are known as powerful antidotes to modern-day stress. Who hasn't enjoyed unwinding and meditatively knitting on a Saturday afternoon with a freshly-brewed cup of tea by her side? Knitting and tea also form a combination that inspires socializing—many knitters take great pleasure in bringing their latest project along to a cafe where they can meet with friends and partake in a delicious tea, perhaps with cake, sandwich, or pastry while knitting between mouthfuls! Knitting and tea also offer comfort. Most knitters would agree that nothing soothes them like their favorite knitting needles and some soft, gorgeous wool.

This book combines two activities that I am passionate about. My fascination with tea rooms and tea gardens began as a little girl in the United Kingdom when my parents took my sister Sarah and me out for tea. We both adored sampling the delights of various tea rooms and even devised a scoring system for the different establishments we visited, giving them scores out of 10 for the quality of the tea, the cakes, waitress service, and general ambience. As for the knitting part—I have been involved with knitting since the foundation of Artwork, the knitwear company I started with my husband, Patrick, in 1977.

Tea drinking persists across centuries and cultures. This elegant teahouse is in Shanghai, China.

Tea also plays a big part in Patrick's family history. As a little boy, he and his brother, Christopher, were brought up on a tea plantation in Sri Lanka. The first three chapters of *Knitting and Tea* are photographed on the tea plantations of Sri Lanka, and they bring a little bit of Patrick's childhood memories to the book. The remaining chapters are photographed on location in England and bring back memories of my family teas.

In keeping with the wistful, evocative feel of this book, the styling is deliberately retro and many of the garments accompanying our designs are vintage. In each chapter, I have also included a recipe from the chef of the featured establishment that I hope you enjoy.

What could be more perfect than celebrating these two traditions in a book? So it is with much pleasure that I bring you *Knitting and Tea.*

chapter one

CEYLON TEA

All aboard the train to the Hill Country, escaping the heat and dust of Colombo, armed with a picnic rug, sun hat, and knits suitable for colder climes. The travelers look forward to enjoying a picnic tea fanned by the cool breezes in the mountainous tea-planting region of Sri Lanka called Newara Eliya, nearly 6,000 feet (1,830 meters) above sea level.

This very same train took my husband, Patrick, on the same journey when he was a small boy living in Sri Lanka. Most European children living in Sri Lanka before independence in 1972 were sent to boarding school in the Hill Country, where the climate was cooler and healthier. Patrick and his older brother, Christopher, would watch their mother wave good-bye at Colombo Fort Railway Station as they set out on their long journey on the "School Train" up to the hill town of Newara Eliya, which translated means "town above the clouds." The journey took all day on a steam train grinding and puffing its way up from sea level to the dizzy heights of the tea plantations.

They changed trains at Kandy (the old capital of the Kandian Kings) to a more powerful engine that could manage the extreme gradients up to Nanu Oya Station, then traveled by taxi for the last leg of the journey to Newara Eliya. Today the journey is faster by diesel train, but the breath-taking views across some of the most beautiful countryside imaginable are still the same. The passage takes you from the flat plains of rice paddy fields, over virgin rain forests and huge snaking rivers, giving way to the intense green hills of the tea plantations, only interrupted by the brilliant colors of the clothes worn by the women tea-pickers.

The view of tea plantations at dawn

My father-in-law, John Gottelier, was an English tea planter in Sri Lanka (or Ceylon, as it was then known), as were his relatives going back two more generations. Originally, his great-grandfather and Patrick's great-great-grandfather came to Sri Lanka to plant coffee, but this was short-lived due to the great coffee blight of 1869 that destroyed all the coffee grown on the island. Luckily, the introduction of tea to Sri Lanka followed very shortly afterward and is generally attributed to one James Taylor, a Scottish farm boy who worked his way up to becoming a planter. After the coffee blight, he experimented with different tea seedlings acquired from the Botanical Gardens at Kandy, and he grew them on the long veranda of his estate bungalow. The seedlings flourished and were harvested and processed. The result was a most delicious tea. Taylor's Planter's Bungalow became a mecca for those coffee planters who wanted to know how to grow and process tea.

As interest in his tea business grew, he built a teahouse out of local rock, which became the first tea factory in Sri Lanka. From Taylor's humble experiments in tea growing, Sri Lanka has grown into the third largest tea exporter in the world. The tea plantations today are now owned and run by Sri Lankans, who export probably the finest tea in the world, known to us as Ceylon tea.

The Five Golden Rules
for Making the Perfect Cup of Tea

1. Use high-quality tea. Keep the tea in an airtight container.
2. Use fresh water that has just reached the state of bubbling fiercely.
3. Always preheat the teapot.
4. Take the teapot to the kettle and not the kettle to the teapot.
5. Let the tea stand between 4 and 5 minutes. Stir the tea in the pot, before pouring out.

—*The Tea Factory, Kandapola, Newara Eliya*

TOP: The Tea factory at dawn.

BOTTOM: Tea field information marker.

CEYLON CARDIGAN

Skill level: Easy.

Size: XS(S, M, L, XL, XXL).

Finished Bust 32¼(36¼, 40, 44, 48½, 52¾)" (82[92, 102, 112, 123, 134]cm).

Materials:

5(5, 6, 6, 7, 7) skeins Blue Sky Alpacas Royal Alpaca, 100% Royal Alpaca [3½ oz (100g), 288yd (263m)], Seaglass. fine
Remnants of other yarns for embroidery (optional—we used Blue Sky Alpacas Alpaca / Silk in colors Ruby, Blush, Peacock, Spring, and Plum).
Size 3 (3.25mm) and 5 (3.75mm) straight needles. Size 3 (3.25mm) 16" (40.5mm) circular needle for front edgings.

Gauge: 24 stitches and 28 rows to 4" (10cm) over stockinette stitch on 3.75mm needles.

Back

Cast on 122(134, 146, 158, 172, 184) stitches using size 3 (3.25mm) needles. Work 4 rows seed stitch, change to size 5 (3.75mm) needles and continue in stockinette stitch with purl dot rows as follows:

Row 1: K23(25, 27, 29, 31, 33), p1, k23(25, 27, 29, 31, 33) p1 k26(30, 34, 38, 44, 48), p1, k23(25, 27, 29, 31, 33), p1, k23(25, 27, 29, 31, 33).

Row 2 (and all wrong-side rows): Purl.

Repeat these 2 rows until back measures 3¼"(3¼, 3¼, 3½, 3½, 3¾)" (8[8, 8, 9, 9, 9.5]cm) from cast-on edge.

First decrease row: K23(25, 27, 29, 31, 33), p1, ssk, k21(23, 25, 27, 29, 31), p1, ssk, k22(26, 30, 34, 40, 44), k2tog, p1, k21(23, 25, 27, 29, 31), k2tog, k23(25, 27, 29, 31, 33). 118(130, 142, 154, 168, 180) stitches.

Work 9 rows even, keeping continuity of purl dot pattern.

Second decrease row: K23(25, 27, 29, 31, 33), p1, ssk, k20(22, 24, 26, 28, 30), p1, ssk, k20(24, 28, 32, 38, 42), k2tog, p1, k20(22, 24, 26, 28, 30), k2tog, p1, k23(25, 27, 29, 31, 33). 114(126, 138, 150, 164, 176) stitches.

Work 9 rows even, keeping continuity of purl dot pattern.

Third decrease row: K23(25, 27, 29, 31, 33), p1, ssk, k19(21, 23, 25, 27, 29), p1, ssk, k18(22, 26, 30, 26, 40), k2tog, p1, k19(21, 23, 25, 27, 29), k2tog, p1, k23(25, 27, 29, 31, 33). 110(122, 134, 146, 160, 172) stitches.

Work 9 rows even.

Work decrease rows as set (decreasing 4 stitches on each row) on next and following 10th rows twice, 6 decrease rows worked in total. 98(110, 122, 134, 148, 160) stitches. Work even, keeping purl dot pattern correct until back measures 15(15½, 15½, 15¾, 15¾, 16)" (38[39.5, 39.5, 40, 40, 41]cm) from cast-on edge with right side facing for next row.

Decrease for armholes (keeping purl dot pattern correct)

X-Small: Bind off 2 stitches at the beginning of the next 4 rows, then 1 stitch at the beginning of the following 2 rows. 88 stitches. Work even until the armhole measures 2¾"(7cm), stop working the 2 outside purl dot patterns. Work even for a further 2"(5cm), now stop working the 2 remaining purl dot patterns. Work even in stockinette stitch until the armhole measures 8"(20.5cm) in total.

Small: Bind off 4 stitches at the beginning of the next 2 rows, then 3 stitches at the beginning of the following 2 rows, then 2 stitches, then 1 stitch at each end of the next right-side row. 90 stitches. Work even until armhole measures 3"(7.5cm), stop working the 2 outside purl dot rows. Work even for a further 2"(5cm), now stop working the 2 remaining purl dot patterns. Work even in stockinette stitch until the armhole measures 8"(20.5cm) total.

Medium: Bind off 4 stitches at the beginning of the next 2 rows, then 3 stitches at the beginning of the following 2 rows, then 2 stitches, then 1 stitch at each end of the next 2 right-side rows. 100 stitches. Work even until armhole measures 3"(7.5cm), stop working the 2 outside purl dot rows. Work even for a further 2"(5cm), stop working the 2 remaining purl dot patterns. Work even in stockinette stitch until the armhole measures 8"(20.5cm) total.

Large: Bind off 4 stitches at the beginning of the next 2 rows, then 3 stitches at the beginning of the following 2 rows, then 2 stitches at the beginning of the following 4 rows, then 1 stitch at each end of the next 3 right-side rows. 106 stitches. Work even until armhole measures 3"(7.5cm), stop working the 2 outside purl dot rows. Work even for a further 2"(5cm), stop working the 2 remaining purl dot patterns. Work even in stockinette stitch until the armhole measures 8¾"(22cm) total.

X-Large: Bind off 4 stitches at the beginning of the next 2 rows, then 3 stitches at the beginning of the following 4 rows, then 2 stitches at the beginning of the following 6 rows, then 1 stitch at each end of the next 5 right-side rows. 106 stitches. Work even until armhole measures 3¾"(9.5cm), stop working the 2 outside purl dot rows. Work even for a further 2½"(6.5cm), stop working the 2 remaining purl dot patterns. Work even in stockinette stitch until the armhole measures 9"(23cm) total.

XX-Large: Bind off 5 stitches at the beginning of the next 2 rows, then 4 stitches at the beginning of the next 2 rows, then 3 stitches at the beginning of the following 4 rows, then 2 stitches at the beginning of the following 4 rows, then 1 stitch at each end of the next 6 right-side rows. 110 stitches. Work even until armhole measures 4"(10cm), stop working the 2 outside purl dot rows. Work even for a further 2½"(6cm), stop working the 2 remaining purl dot patterns. Work even in stockinette stitch until the armhole measures 9½"(24cm) total.

Shape shoulders

Bind off 9(10, 10, 11, 11, 12) stitches at the beginning of the next row, knit 19(19, 21, 23, 23, 25), turn. 20(20, 22, 24, 24, 26) stitches on needle.

Row 1: P2tog, p to end.

Row 2: Bind off 9(9, 10, 11, 11, 12) stitches, k to last 2 stitches, k2tog.

Row 3: Purl.

Row 4: Bind off remaining 9(9, 10, 11, 11, 11) stitches.

Rejoin yarn to remaining stitches, bind off central 30(30, 36, 36, 36, 36) stitches, knit to end.

Row 1: Bind off 9(9, 10, 11, 11, 12) stitches, p to last 2 stitches, p2tog.

Row 2: K2tog, k to end.

Row 3: Bind off remaining 9(9, 10, 11, 11, 11) stitches.

Left front

Cast on 61(67, 73, 79, 86, 92) stitches using size 3(3.25mm) needles. Work 4 rows seed stitch, change to size 5 (3.75mm) needles and begin stockinette stitch and purl dot pattern:

Row 1: K23(25, 27, 29, 31, 33), p1, k20(22, 24, 26, 28, 30), p1, k16(18, 20, 22, 25, 27).

Row 2: Purl.

Work even in pattern as set until front measures 3¼"(3¼, 3¼, 3½, 3½, 3¾)" (8[8, 8, 9, 9, 9.5]cm) from cast-on edge, begin decreasing:

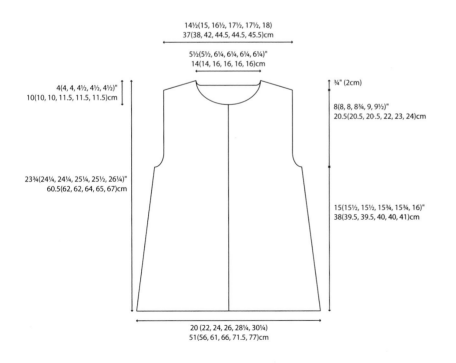

14½(15, 16½, 17½, 17½, 18)
37(38, 42, 44.5, 44.5, 45.5)cm

5½(5½, 6¼, 6¼, 6¼, 6¼)"
14(14, 16, 16, 16, 16)cm

4(4, 4½, 4½, 4½)"
10(10, 10, 11.5, 11.5, 11.5)cm

¾" (2cm)

8(8, 8¾, 9, 9½)"
20.5(20.5, 20.5, 22, 23, 24)cm

23¾(24¼, 24¼, 25¼, 25½, 26¼)"
60.5(62, 62, 64, 65, 67)cm

15(15½, 15½, 15¾, 15¾, 16)"
38(39.5, 39.5, 40, 40, 41)cm

20 (22, 24, 26, 28¼, 30¼)
51(56, 61, 66, 71.5, 77)cm

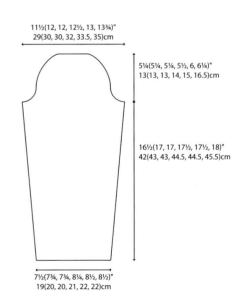

11½(12, 12, 12½, 13, 13¾)"
29(30, 30, 32, 33.5, 35)cm

5¼(5¼, 5¼, 5½, 6, 6¼)"
13(13, 13, 14, 15, 16.5)cm

16½(17, 17, 17½, 17½, 18)"
42(43, 43, 44.5, 44.5, 45.5)cm

7½(7¾, 7¾, 8¼, 8½, 8½)"
19(20, 20, 21, 22, 22)cm

First decrease row: K23(25, 27, 29, 31, 33), p1, ssk, k18(20, 22, 24, 26, 28), p1, ssk, k14(16, 18, 20, 23, 25). 59(65, 71, 77, 84, 90) stitches. Work 9 rows even.

Second decrease row: K23(25, 27, 29, 31, 33), p1, ssk, k17(19, 21, 23, 25, 27) p1, ssk, k13(15, 17, 19, 22, 24). 57(63, 69, 75, 82, 88) stitches. Work 9 rows even.

Third decrease row: K23(25, 27, 29, 31, 33), p1, ssk, k16(18, 20, 22, 24, 26) p1, ssk, k12(14, 16, 18, 21, 23). 55(61, 67, 73, 80, 86) stitches. Work 3 more decrease rows (decreasing 2 stitches each time) as set with 9 rows between each decrease row. 49(55, 61, 67, 74, 80) stitches.

Work even, keeping purl dot pattern correct until front measures 15(15½, 15½, 15¾, 15¾, 16)" (38[39.5, 39.5, 40, 40, 41]cm) from cast-on edge with right side facing for next row.

Decrease for armholes (keeping purl dot pattern correct)

X-Small: Bind off 2 stitches at the beginning of the next 2 right-side rows, then 1 stitch at the beginning of the following right-side row. 44 stitches. Work even until the armhole measures 2¾"(7cm), stop working BOTH purl dot patterns. Work even until front armhole is 4" (10cm) shorter than back armhole, with the wrong side of work facing for next row to begin front neck shaping:

Next row: Bind off 4 stitches at the beginning of the next row, then bind off 4, 3, 2, 2, 1, 1 stitches at the beginning of the following 6 wrong-side rows. 27 stitches. Work even until front armhole matches back armhole to the beginning of shoulder shaping, right side facing for next row. Bind off 9 stitches at the beginning of the next 3 right-side rows.

Small: Bind off 4 stitches at the beginning of the next row, then 3, 2, 1 stitches at the beginning of the next 3 right-side rows. 45 stitches. Work even until armhole measures 3"(7.5cm), stop working BOTH purl dot patterns. Work even until front armhole is 4" (10cm) shorter than back armhole, with the wrong side of work facing for next row to begin front neck shaping:

Next row: Bind off 4 stitches at the beginning of the next row, then bind off 4, 3, 2, 1, 1 stitches at the beginning of the following 6 wrong-side rows. 28 stitches. Work even until front armhole matches back armhole to the beginning of shoulder shaping, right side facing for next row. Bind off 10, 9, 9 stitches at the beginning of the next 3 right-side rows.

Medium: Bind off 4 stitches at the beginning of the next row, then 3, 2, 1, 1 stitches at the beginning of the next 4 right-side rows. 50 stitches. Work even until armhole measures 3"(7.5cm), stop working BOTH purl dot patterns. Work even until front armhole is 4" (10cm) shorter than back armhole, with the wrong side of work facing for next row to begin front neck shaping:

Next row: Bind off 4 stitches at the beginning of the next row, then bind off 4, 3, 2, 2, 1, 1, 1 stitches at the beginning of the following 8 wrong-side rows. 30 stitches. Work even until front armhole matches back armhole to the beginning of shoulder shaping, right side facing for next row. Bind off 10 stitches at the beginning of the next 3 right-side rows.

Large: Bind off 4 stitches at the beginning of the next row, then bind off 3, 2, 2, 1, 1, 1 stitches at the beginning of the following 6 right-side rows. 53 stitches. Work even until armhole measures 3"(7.5cm), stop working BOTH purl dot patterns. Work even until front armhole is 4½" (11.5cm) shorter than back armhole, with the wrong side of work facing for next row to begin front neck shaping:

Next row: Bind off 4 stitches at the beginning of the next row, then bind off 4, 3, 2, 2, 2, 1, 1, 1 stitches at the beginning of the following 8 wrong-side rows. 33 stitches. Work even until front armhole matches back armhole to the beginning of shoulder shaping, right side facing for next row. Bind off 11 stitches at the beginning of the next 3 right-side rows.

X-Large: Bind off 4 stitches at the beginning of the next row, then bind off 3, 3, 2, 2, 2, 1, 1, 1, 1 stitches at the beginning of the following 10 right-side rows. 53 stitches. AT THE SAME TIME, when armhole measures 3½"(9cm), stop working BOTH purl dot patterns. Work even until front armhole is 4½" (11.5cm) shorter than back armhole, with the wrong side of work facing for next row to begin front neck shaping:

Next row: Bind off 4 stitches at sthe beginning of the next row, then bind off 4, 3, 2, 2, 1, 1, 1 stitches at the beginning of the following 8 wrong-side rows. 33 stitches. Work even until front armhole matches back armhole to the beginning of shoulder shaping, right side facing for next row. Bind off 11 stitches at the beginning of the next 3 right-side rows.

XX-Large: Bind off 5 stitches at the beginning of the next row, then bind off 4, 3, 3, 2, 2, 1, 1, 1, 1, 1 stitches at the beginning of the following 11 right-side rows. 55 stitches. AT THE SAME TIME, when armhole measures 3½"(9cm), stop working BOTH purl dot patterns. Work even until front armhole is 4½" (11.5cm) shorter than back armhole, with the wrong side of work facing for next row to begin front neck shaping:

Next row: Bind off 4 stitches at the beginning of the next row, then bind off 4, 3, 2, 2, 2, 1, 1, 1 stitches at the beginning of the following 8 wrong-side rows. 35 stitches. Work even until front armhole matches back armhole to the beginning of

Row 3: K14(16, 18, 20, 23, 25), k2tog, p1, k18(20, 22, 24, 26, 28), k2tog, p1, k23(25, 27, 29, 31, 33). 59(65, 71, 77, 84, 90) stitches.

Work 9 rows even.

First decrease row: K13(15, 17, 19, 22, 24), k2tog, p1, k17(19, 21, 23, 25, 27), k2tog, p1, k23(25, 27, 29, 31, 33). 57(63, 69, 75, 82, 88) stitches.

Work 9 rows even.

Second decrease row: K12(14, 16, 18, 21, 23), k2tog, p1, k16(18, 20, 22, 24, 26), k2tog, p1, k23(25, 27, 29, 31, 33). 55(61, 67, 73, 80, 86) stitches.

Work 3 more decrease rows (decreasing 2 stitches each time) as set with 9 rows between each decrease row. 49(55, 61, 67, 74, 80) stitches.

Work even, keeping purl dot pattern correct until front measures 15(15½, 15½, 15¾, 15¾, 16)" (38[39.5, 39.5, 40, 40, 41]cm) from cast-on edge with wrong side facing for next row.

Decrease for armholes (keeping purl dot pattern correct)
X-Small: Bind off 2 stitches at the beginning of the next 2 wrong-side rows, then 1 stitch at the beginning of the following wrong-side row. 44 stitches. Work even until the armhole measures 2¾" (7cm), stop working BOTH purl dot patterns. Work even until front armhole is 4" (10cm) shorter than back armhole, with the right side of work facing for next row to begin front neck shaping:
Next row: Bind off 4 stitches at the beginning of the next row, then bind off 4, 3, 2, 2, 1, 1 stitches at the beginning of the following 6 right-side rows. 27 stitches. Work even until front armhole matches back armhole to the beginning of shoulder shaping, wrong side facing for next row. Bind off 9 stitches at the beginning of the next 3 wrong-side rows.
Small: Bind off 4 stitches at the beginning of the next row, then 3, 2, 1 stitches at the beginning of the next 3 wrong-side rows. 45 stitches. Work even until armhole measures 3" (7.5cm), stop working BOTH purl dot patterns. Work even until front armhole is 4" (10cm) shorter than back armhole, with the right side of work facing for next row to begin front neck shaping:
Next row: Bind off 4 stitches at the beginning of the next row, then bind off 4, 3, 2, 2, 1, 1 stitches at the beginning of the following 6 right-side rows. 28 stitches. Work even until front armhole matches back armhole to the beginning of shoulder shaping, wrong side facing for next row. Bind off 10, 9, 9 stitches at the beginning of the next 3 wrong-side rows.
Medium: Bind off 4 stitches at the beginning of the next row, then 3, 2, 1, 1 stitches

shoulder shaping, right side facing for next row. Bind off 12, 12, 11 stitches at the beginning of the next 3 right-side rows.

Right front
Cast on 61(67, 73, 79, 86, 92) stitches using size 3(3.25mm) needles. Work 4 rows seed stitch, change to size 5 (3.75mm) needles and begin stockinette stitch and purl dot pattern:
Row 1: K16(18, 20, 22, 25, 27) p1, k20(22, 24, 26, 28, 30), p1, k23(25, 27, 29, 31, 33).
Row 2: Purl.
Work even in pattern as set until front measures 3¼"(3¼, 3¼, 3½, 3½, 3¾)" (8[8, 8, 9, 9, 9.5]cm) from cast-on edge, begin decreasing:

at the beginning of the next 4 wrong-side rows. 50 stitches. Work even until armhole measures 3" (7.5cm), stop working BOTH purl dot patterns. Work even until front armhole is 4" (10cm) shorter than back armhole, with the right side of work facing for next row to begin front neck shaping:

Next row: Bind off 4 stitches at the beginning of the next row, then bind off 4, 3, 2, 2, 2, 1, 1, 1 stitches at the beginning of the following 8 right-side rows. 30 stitches. Work even until front armhole matches back armhole to the beginning of shoulder shaping, wrong side facing for next row. Bind off 10 stitches at the beginning of the next 3 wrong-side rows.

Large: Bind off 4 stitches at the beginning of the next row, then 3, 2, 2, 1, 1, 1 stitches at the beginning of the next 6 wrong-side rows. 53 stitches. Work even until armhole measures 3" (7.5cm), stop working BOTH purl dot patterns. Work even until front armhole is 4½" (11.5cm) shorter than back armhole, with the right side of work facing for next row to begin front neck shaping:

Next row: Bind off 4 stitches at the beginning of the next row, then bind off 4, 3, 2, 2, 2, 1, 1, 1 stitches at the beginning of the following 8 right-side rows. 33 stitches. Work even until front armhole matches back armhole to the beginning of shoulder shaping, wrong side facing for next row. Bind off 11 stitches at the beginning of the next 3 wrong-side rows.

X-Large: Bind off 4 stitches at the beginning of the next row, then 3, 3, 2, 2, 2, 1, 1, 1, 1, 1 stitches at the beginning of the next 10 wrong-side rows. 53 stitches. AT THE SAME TIME, when armhole measures 3½" (9cm), stop working BOTH purl dot patterns. Work even until front armhole is 4½" (11.5cm) shorter than back armhole, with the right side of work facing for next row to begin front neck shaping:

Next row: Bind off 4 stitches at the beginning of the next row, then bind off 4, 3, 2, 2, 2, 1, 1, 1 stitches at the beginning of the following 8 right-side rows. 33 stitches. Work even until front armhole matches back armhole to the beginning of shoulder shaping, wrong side facing for next row. Bind off 11 stitches at the beginning of the next 3 wrong-side rows.

XX-Large: Bind off 5 stitches at the beginning of the next row, then 4, 3, 3, 2, 2, 1, 1, 1, 1, 1, 1 stitches at the beginning of the next 11 wrong-side rows. 55 stitches. AT THE SAME TIME, when armhole measures 3½" (9cm), stop working BOTH purl dot patterns. Work even until front armhole is 4½" (11.5cm) shorter than back armhole, with the right side of work facing for next row to begin front neck shaping:

Next row: Bind off 4 stitches at the beginning of the next row, then bind off 4, 3, 2, 2, 2, 1, 1, 1 stitches at the beginning of the following 8 right-side rows. 35 stitches.

Work even until front armhole matches back armhole to the beginning of shoulder shaping, wrong side facing for next row. Bind off 12, 12, 11 stitches at the beginning of the next 3 wrong-side rows.

Sleeves

Cast on 46(50, 50, 52, 54, 54) stitches using size 3 (3.25mm) needles and work 4 rows seed stitch. Change to size 5 (3.75mm) needles and work in stockinette stitch from now on. Work 8 rows, increase on 9th row:

Next row: K2, m1, k to last 2 stitches, m1, k2.

X-Small, Small, and Medium: Increase on every following 10th row 9 times more, then once on the following 8th row, then once on the following 6th row. 70(74, 74) stitches. Work even until sleeve measures 16½"(17, 17)" (42[43, 43]cm) from cast-on edge.

Large, X-Large: Increase on every following 8th row 12(13) times more. 78(82) stitches. Work even until sleeve measures 17½(17½)" from cast-on edge.

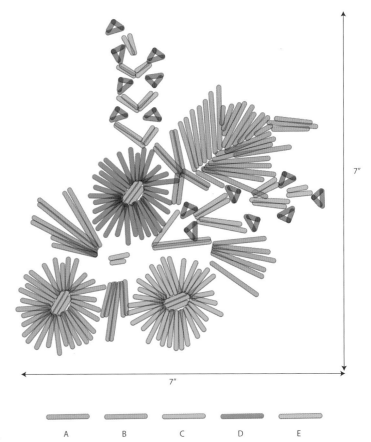

7"

7"

A   B   C   D   E

XX-Large: Increase on every following *8th, then 6th row, repeat from * 7 times, then increase on following 8th row once more. 86 stitches. Work even until sleeve measures 18" from cast-on edge.

Shape sleeve cap

X-Small, Small, and Medium: Bind off 4 stitches at the beginning of the next 2 rows, then 3 stitches at the beginning of the following 2 rows, then 2 stitches at the beginning of the next 2 rows, then decrease 1 stitch at each end of the next 14 right-side rows. Now bind off 2 stitches at the beginning of the next 4 rows, bind off the remaining 20 stitches. Sleeve cap should measure approximately 5¼" (13cm) from the beginning of shaping.

Large: Bind off 4 stitches at the beginning of the next 2 rows, then 3 stitches at the beginning of the following 2 rows, then 2 stitches at the beginning of the next 4 rows, then decrease 1 stitch at each end of the next 14 right-side rows. Now bind off 2 stitches at the beginning of the next 4 rows, bind off the remaining 22 stitches. Sleeve cap should measure approximately 5½" (14cm) from the beginning of shaping.

X-Large: Bind off 4 stitches at the beginning of the next 2 rows, then 3 stitches at the beginning of the following 4 rows, then 2 stitches at the beginning of the next 4 rows. Work 2 rows even, decrease 1 stitch at each end of the next 15 right-side rows, bind off the remaining 24 stitches. Sleeve cap should measure approximately 6" (15cm).

XX-Large: Bind off 5 stitches at the beginning of the next 2 rows, then 4 stitches at the beginning of the following 2 rows, then 3 stitches at the beginning of the next 2 rows. Now bind off 2 stitches at the beginning of the following 4 rows. Work 2 rows even. * Decrease 1 stitch at each end of the next row, work 3 rows even, repeat from * once more. Decrease 1 stitch at each end of the next 12 right-side rows, bind off the remaining 26 stitches. Sleeve cap should measure approximately 6¼" (16cm).

Front edgings (both alike)

With the right side of front facing and size 3 (3.25mm) circular needle, pick up and knit 2 stitches for every 3 rows worked on the front from the hem to the beginning of the neck shaping. Break yarn, leaving enough at each end to weave in neatly. With a separate ball of yarn and again with the right side of the front facing, cast on 3 stitches. Work 3-stitch applied I-cord border along length of the front. Sew shoulder seams.

Neckband and ties

Cast on 3 stitches using size 3 (3.25mm) needles. Work 2 rows seed stitch.

Next row: Keeping continuity of seed stitch, pattern 2, kfb. 4 stitches.

Next row: Work in seed stitch.

Repeat Rows 3 and 4 until you have 7 stitches, then work even until the longer side of the tie measures 22" (56cm), with the right side of the tie facing. Increase 1 stitch as before at the end of the next 2 right-side rows. 9 stitches. Mark the right side of the work with a safety pin or tie a small loop of yarn around a stitch. Begin neckband, working in bias pattern from now on to help it lie neatly when you sew it on:

Row 1: In pattern, pattern 1, pattern 2 together, work in pattern to last stitch, kfb or pfb, depending on pattern.

Next row: Pattern. As you have increased at the end of the last row and decreased at the beginning of it, then this row will not work exactly in seed stitch, but if you keep the beginning of the row correct and just pattern across, not minding if you work 1 stitch in rib at the end of the row, it will look fine.

Next row: This is where you put the seed stitch right. Work even in pattern.

Next row: Work even in pattern.

Repeat these 4 rows until neckband fits neatly around neck up left front, across the back and down the right front, ending ¼" (6mm) before right front neck shaping ends, with right side of neckband facing for decrease row:

Next row: Pattern 2 together, work in pattern to end.

Next row: Work even in pattern. Repeat these 2 rows once more. 7 stitches. Mark the right side of the tie here.

Work even on these 7 stitches for front tie until it measures the same as the shorter edge of the other tie, right side facing. Repeat the decrease row above and the even row until 3 stitches remain, bind off.

Slip stitch the tie around neck shaping on the body, placing marked points at the beginning and end of neck shaping.

Finishing

Sew side and sleeve seams, set in sleeves and weave in all ends.

Embroidery

Using diagram as reference for colors and placement, embroider flowers and leaves using straight stitches and French knots.

Skill level: Intermediate.

Size: Age 2(4, 6, 8) years.

Finished Chest: 24(26, 28, 30)" (61[66, 71, 76]cm).

Materials:

8(8, 9, 9) balls RYC Cashsoft 4 ply, 57% Extra Fine Merino Wool, 33% Microfiber, 10% Cashmere [1¾ oz (50g), 197yd (180m)], 3(3, 4, 4) balls in Savannah (MC), 1 ball each of Poppy, Kiwi, Walnut, Forest, and Bark. **(1)** super fine

Size 2 (2.75mm) and 3 (3.25mm) needles, or size needed to obtain gauge.

Gauge: 30½ stitches and 31 rows to 4" (10cm) over Fair Isle pattern on 3.25mm needles.

Front

Cast on 93(101, 107, 115) stitches using size 2 (2.75mm) needles and MC and work 1½(1½, 2, 2)" (3.8[3.8, 5, 5]cm) in k1, p1 rib. Change to size 3 (3.25mm) needles and work Fair Isle pattern from chart in stockinette stitch until front measures 10(11, 12½,14½)" (25.5[28, 32, 37]cm) from cast-on edge. Shape armholes and front neck:

Bind off 4 stitches at the beginning of the next row, knit 41(45, 48, 52) stitches (42[46, 49, 53] stitches on right-hand needle), turn. Leave remaining stitches on a holder for the right side of the front. Purl the next row in pattern. Now bind off 3 stitches at the beginning of the next row, then 2 stitches on the next right-side row, and 1 stitch at the armhole edge on the next 4(4, 4, 6) right-side rows. AT THE SAME TIME, decrease 1 stitch at the neck edge (by knitting 2 stitches together) on the same row as you bind off 2 stitches at the armhole, and continue to decrease 1 stitch at the neck edge on every right-side row until you have 20(16, 18, 19) stitches left. For the smallest size ONLY decrease 1 stitch at the neck edge on every 3rd row 4 times. 16(16, 18, 19) stitches. Work even until armhole measures 5½(5¾, 6, 6½)" (14[14.5, 15, 16]cm), ending with the right side facing for the next row.

Next row: Bind off 5(5, 6, 6) stitches at the beginning of the row.

Next row: Decrease 1 stitch at the beginning of the row. Bind off 5(5, 6, 6) stitches at the beginning of next row.

Next row: Decrease 0(1, 1, 1) stitches at the beginning of the row. Bind off the remaining 5(5, 5, 6) stitches at the beginning of the next row.

Rejoin yarn to the remaining 47(51, 54, 58) stitches and pattern across. Bind off 4 stitches at the beginning of the next row and place the last stitch of this row onto a holder for the neckband. Work 1 row even. Bind off 3 stitches at the beginning of the next (wrong side) row, then 2 stitches at the armhole edge, then 1 stitch at the armhole edge on the next 4(4, 4, 6) wrong-side rows. AT THE SAME TIME, decrease 1 stitch at the neck edge (by knitting 2 stitches together) on the row after you bind off 3 stitches at the armhole, and continue to decrease 1 stitch at the neck edge on every right-side row until you have 20(16, 18, 19) stitches left. For the smallest size ONLY, decrease 1 stitch at the neck edge on every 3rd row 4 times. 16(16, 18, 19) stitches. Work even until the armhole measures 5½(5¾, 6, 6½)" (14[14.5, 15, 16]cm), ending with the wrong side facing for the next row.

Next row: Bind off 5(5, 6, 6) stitches at the beginning of the row.

Next row: Decrease 1 stitch at the beginning of the row. Bind off 5(5, 6, 6) stitches at the beginning of the next row.

Next row: Decrease 0(1, 1, 1) stitches at the beginning of the row. Bind off the remaining 5(5, 5, 6) stitches at the beginning of the next row.

Back

Cast on 93(101, 107, 115) stitches using size 2 (2.75mm) needles and MC and work 1½(1½, 2, 2)" (3.8[3.8, 5, 5]cm) in k1, p1 rib. Change to size 3 (3.25mm) needles and stockinette stitch and work even until back measures 10(11, 12½,14½)" (25.5[28, 32, 37]cm) from cast-on edge. Shape armholes:

Bind off 4 stitches at the beginning of the next 2 rows, then 3 stitches at the beginning of the following 2 rows, then 2 stitches at the beginning of the next 2 rows, then decrease 1 stitch at each end of the next 4(4, 4, 6) rows. 67(75, 81, 85) stitches. Work even until the armholes measure 5½(5¾, 6, 6½)" (14[14.5, 15, 16]cm), bind off 5(5, 6, 6) stitches at the beginning of the next 4 rows, then bind off 5(5, 5, 6) stitches at the beginning of the next 2 rows. Place the remaining 37(45, 47, 49) stitches on a holder for the back neck.

Neckband

Join right shoulder seam. With the right side of work facing, using size 2 (2.75mm) needles and MC, pick up and knit 38(42, 44, 46) stitches down the left front neck, 1 stitch from holder at center of the front neck (mark this stitch), 38(42, 44, 46) stitches up the right side of neck and rib across the 37(45, 47, 49) stitches held for the back neck, starting with a knit stitch. 114(130, 136, 142) stitches.

Next row: Work in k1, p1 rib.

Next row: Rib to 2 stitches before the marked stitch, ssk, knit the marked stitch, k2tog, rib to end. Work 1 row even.

Repeat these 2 rows (the decrease row and the even row) twice more, work the decrease row once more, bind off in rib.

Right armband

With the right side of work facing and using size 2 (2.75mm) needles and MC, pick up and knit 41(43, 45, 49) stitches from the back armhole shaping to the shoulder and 41(43, 45, 49) stitches down the right front to the armhole. 82(86, 90, 98) stitches. Work 8 rows in k1, p1 rib, bind off in rib. Join left shoulder.

Left armband

With the right side of work facing and using size 2 (2.75mm) needles and MC, pick up and knit 41(43, 45, 49) stitches from the front armhole shaping to the shoulder and 41(43, 45, 49) stitches down the back to the armhole. 82(86, 90, 98) stitches. Work 8 rows in k1, p1 rib, bind off in rib.

Finishing

Join side seams and weave in all ends.

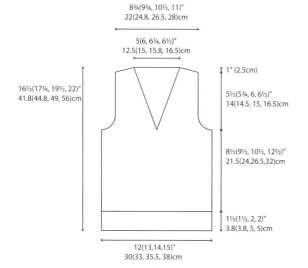

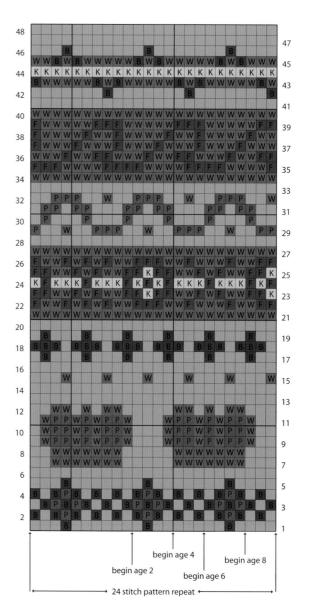

FLOWERDEW EVENING TANK

Skill level: Intermediate

Size: XS (S, M, L)

Finished bust: 30½(32, 35½, 38)" (77.5[81, 90.5, 97]cm)

Materials:

4(4, 5, 5) balls Karabella Yarns Lace Merino, 100% Merino Wool [1¾ oz (50g), 255yd (235m)], Champagne. lace

Approximately 1,150(1,600, 1,650, 1,700) ⅛"(3mm) silver beads.

Size 3(3.25mm) and 2(2.75mm) 20"(51cm) circular needles.

Gauge: 34 stitches and 44 rows to 4"(10cm) over beaded twig pattern.

Body

Thread approximately 198(220, 242, 264) beads onto yarn.

Cast on 252(280, 308, 336) stitches using size 3 (3.25mm) circular needles and join into a round. Mark this join. Work beaded leaf edging:

Round 1: *P5, yo, k1, yo, p5, p3tog, repeat from * around.

Round 2: Knit.

Round 3: P1 *p5, yo, k1, yo, p5, p3tog, repeat from * around. Note the "p1" worked at the beginning of the round becomes the last stitch of the final "p3" of the round. Repeat rounds 2 and 3 4 more times, then round 2 again. 12 rounds worked in total.

Round 13: P1 *p3, yo, k2tog, yo, k1, yo, ssk, yo, p3, p3tog, repeat from * around. Note again the "p1" worked at the beginning of the round becomes the last stitch of the final "p3" of the round.

Round 14 (and all even rounds from now on until stated otherwise): Knit.

Round 15: P1, *p2, yo, k2tog, (k1, yo) twice, k1, ssk, yo, p2, p3tog, repeat from * around. Note again the "p1" worked at the beginning of the round becomes the last stitch of the final "p3" of the round.

Round 17: P1, *p1, yo, k2tog, k2, yo, k1, yo, k2, ssk, yo, p1, p3tog, repeat from * around. Note again the "p1" worked at the beginning of the round becomes the last stitch of the final "p3" of the round.

Round 19: P1, *yo, k2tog, k3, yo, k1, yo, k3, ssk, yo, p3tog, repeat from * around. Note again the "p1" worked at the beginning of the round becomes the last stitch of the final "p3" of the round.

Round 21: *K1, yo, ssk, k7, k2tog, yo, k1, B1K, repeat from * around.

Round 23: *B1K, k1, yo, ssk, k5, k2tog, yo, B1K, k1, repeat from * around.

Round 25: *K1, B1K, k1, yo, ssk, k3, k2tog, yo, k1, B1K, k2, repeat from * around.

Round 27: *K2, B1K, k1, yo, ssk, k1, k2tog, yo, k1, B1K, k3, repeat from * around.

Round 29: *K3, B1K, k1, yo, slip 1, k2tog, psso, yo, k1, B1K, k4, repeat from * around.

Round 31: *K4, B1K, k3, B1k, k5, repeat from * around.

Round 33: *K6, B1K, k7, repeat from * around.

Round 35: Knit.

Round 36: Knit.

Change to size 2 (2.75mm) circular needle and work 7 rounds of k1, p1 rib. On the next (8th) round, increase or decrease stitches, depending on the size being knitted:

X-Small: *rib 21, m1, repeat from * around. 264 stitches.

Small: Rib 35, m1, rib 35, m1, rib 35, m1, rib 70, m1, rib 35, m1, rib 35, m1, rib 35. 286 stitches.

Medium: Work even. 308 stitches.

Large: *Rib 54, k2tog, repeat from * around. 330 stitches.

Cut yarn, and thread on more beads. There is no point in threading on all the beads needed for the body section as the yarn would become too heavy, so thread on as many as you feel comfortable working with and when these are used, cut the yarn again and thread on more.

Change back to size 3 (3.25mm) needle and work from chart in beaded twig pattern (11-stitch pattern repeat) until the beaded twig section measures 13(13½, 13¾,14¼)"(33[34.5, 35, 36]cm) from the beginning.

Shape armholes

Work back and front separately now. Bind off 4(5, 5, 6) stitches at the beginning of the next round, pattern 127(137, 148, 158) stitches, turn. 128(138, 143, 159)

stitches. Place remaining stitches on a holder, noting which row of the beaded twig pattern you end on.

*Keeping pattern correct, bind off 4(5, 5, 6) stitches at the beginning of the next row, then 3(4, 4, 5) stitches at the beginning of the next 4 rows, then 2(3, 3, 4) stitches on the next 2 rows, then 1(2, 2, 3) stitches on the next 8 rows. 100(95, 106, 101) stitches.

Begin neck shaping

X-Small: Bind off 1 stitch at the beginning of the next row, pattern 28, turn. 29 stitches. **Bind off 5 stitches at the beginning of this next (wrong side) row. Bind off 1 stitch at the beginning of the next row, 5 stitches at the beginning of the next row, and 1 stitch again at the armhole edge at the beginning of the next row. Bind off 5 stitches at the beginning of the next row (neck edge), work 1 row even, bind off 4 stitches at the beginning of the next row. Bind off 1 stitch at the beginning of the next row, 2 at the beginning of the next row, work 1 row even. Bind off 1 stitch at the beginning of the next 3 rows. 2 stitches. Work 2 rows even, bind off. Rejoin yarn to the remaining stitches, bind off the central 40 stitches, work in pattern to the end. Bind off 1 stitch at the beginning of the next row, work in pattern to the end. Work from **. Rejoin yarn to the stitches held for the back, bind off 4 stitches at the beginning of this row, complete back by working as for front from *.

Small: Bind off 1 stitch at the beginning of the next row, pattern 25, turn. 26 stitches. **Bind off 5 stitches at the beginning of this next (wrong side) row. Bind off 1 stitch at the beginning of the next row, 4 stitches at the beginning of the next row, and 1 stitch again at the armhole edge at the beginning of the next row. Bind off 4 stitches at the beginning of the next row, 1 stitch at the beginning of the next, and 3 at the beginning of the next row. Work 1 row even, bind off 2 stitches at the beginning of the next row (neck edge), and 1 stitch at the beginning of the next 2 rows. Work 2 rows even, bind off 1 stitch at the beginning of the next row. 2 stitches. Work 1 row even, bind off.

Rejoin yarn to the remaining stitches, bind off the central 41 stitches, work in pattern to the end. Bind off 1 stitch at the beginning of the next row, work in pattern to the end. Work from **. Rejoin yarn to the stitches held for the back, bind off 5 stitches at the beginning of this row, complete back by working as for front from *.

Medium: Bind off 1 stitch at the beginning of the next row, pattern 30, turn. 31 stitches. **Bind off 5 stitches at the beginning of this next (wrong side) row. Bind

off 1 stitch at the beginning of the next row, 5 stitches at the beginning of the next row, and 1 stitch again at the armhole edge at the beginning of the next row. Bind off 4 stitches at the beginning of the next row, work 1 row even, bind off 4 stitches at the beginning of the following row, 1 stitch at the beginning of the next, and 3 at the beginning of the next row. Work 1 row even, bind off 1 stitch at the beginning of the next row (neck edge), and 1 stitch at the beginning of the next 2 rows. Work 2 rows even, bind off 1 stitch at the beginning of the next row. 2 stitches. Work 2 rows even, bind off.

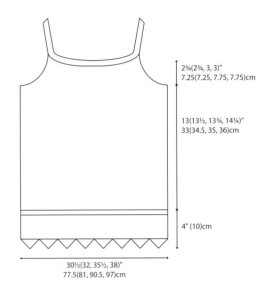

2¾(2¾, 3, 3)"
7.25(7.25, 7.75, 7.75)cm

13(13½, 13¾, 14¼)"
33(34.5, 35, 36)cm

4" (10)cm

30½(32, 35½, 38)"
77.5(81, 90.5, 97)cm

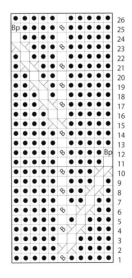

| • | Purl on right side, knit on wrong side |

| ⟋ | Knit through the back of the loop |

Right Twist. Knit 2 together, leaving stitches on left hand needle, then insert right hand needle from the front between the stitches just knitted together, knit the first stitch again and slip both stitches from the needle together.

Left Twist. With right hand needle behind left hand needle, skip one stitch and knit the second stitch in the back of the loop, then insert right hand needle into the backs of both stitches (the skipped stitch and the second stitch) and knit 2 together through the backs of the loops.

Bp — Bead this stitch purlwise. Slide the bead up the yarn close to the last stitch worked, slip the stitch from the left hand needle to the right hand needle so that the bead lies snugly in front of it, and purl the next stitch as usual.

Rejoin yarn to the remaining stitches, bind off the central 44 stitches, work in pattern to the end. Bind off 1 stitch at the beginning of the next row, work in pattern to the end. Work from **. Rejoin yarn to the stitches held for the back, bind off 5 stitches at the beginning of this row, complete back by working as for front from *.

Large: Bind off 1 stitch at the beginning of the next row, pattern 26, turn. 27 stitches. **Bind off 5 stitches at the beginning of this next (wrong side) row. Bind off 1 stitch at the beginning of the next row, 4 stitches at the beginning of the next row, work 1 row even, bind off 4 stitches at the beginning of the following row, work 1 row even, and then bind off 3 stitches at the beginning of the next row. Work 1 row even, bind off 2 stitches at the beginning of the next row (neck edge), and 1 stitch at the beginning of the next row. Work 2 rows even, bind off 1 stitch at the beginning of the next 2 rows, work 2 rows even, bind off 1 stitch at the beginning of the following 2 rows. 3 stitches. Work 1 row even, bind off.

Rejoin yarn to the remaining stitches, bind off the central 49 stitches, work in pattern to the end. Bind off 1 stitch at the beginning of the next row, work in pattern to the end. Work from **. Rejoin yarn to the stitches held for the back, bind off 6 stitches at the beginning of this row, complete back by working as for front from *.

Armhole edgings

Using size 2 (2.75mm) needle, pick up and knit 67 (71, 79, 87) stitches from the top point of the front armhole shaping to the top point of the back armhole shaping (for right trim, from top of back shaping to top of front shaping for left trim). Work 5 rows k1, p1 rib. Bind off in rib.

Neckband

Cast on 231 (237, 241, 247) stitches using size 2 (2.75mm) needle. Knit 1 row. Cut yarn, leaving a long tail. Thread on 229(235, 239, 254) beads.

Next row: K1 *insert needle into the next stitch without knitting it, slip 1 finger from your left hand under the point of the right-hand needle, wrap yarn around your finger and the point of the right-hand needle, AT THE SAME TIME push 1 bead up onto the yarn that forms this loop. Draw the yarn through the stitch on the left-hand needle, put this loop just formed back onto the left-hand needle and knit it and the original stitch together, slipping both loops off the needle at the same time. Repeat from * to the last stitch, k1.

Next row: Knit. Cut yarn, thread on another 229(235, 239, 254) beads. Repeat these 2 rows 4 times more, bind off. Sew edges of neckband together. Place vest on a flat surface and arrange neckband to form even straps, pin onto vest. Sew neckband around neck shaping and edges of armhole trims on front and back.

FLOWERDEW TEA

Flowerdew tea is named after Mr. W. Flowerdew, who founded the Hethersett Tea Estate in 1879. The tea still grown on this upcountry tea plantation in Sri Lanka is where the "Champagne of Teas" originated. Flowerdew tea is made from the finest young tips of the plucked first two leaves and bud, known as the first *flush*. Flowerdew is a type of orange pekoe tea made from the whole leaf, and it is twisted rather than broken. The color of the tea is a delicate pale gold, which denotes its fine quality. This champagne of teas is best consumed without any addition of milk or sugar to really appreciate its subtle flavor.

The Gottelier family, who first came to Sri Lanka a few years before Mr. Flowerdew to plant coffee and later tea, must have shared many similar experiences. As a tea-planting family, they would have lived in a planter's bungalow just like Mr. Flowerdew, who quaintly named his a "cottage." The bungalow no doubt reminded them of home. The original bungalows in Sri Lanka were a hybrid between English manor houses and Indian pavilions. They usually had verandas and terraces as well as English-styled lawns, shrubberies, and flower beds, creating an oasis of the homeland among the vast expanses of tea bushes.

The more affluent planters had very large, grand bungalows, often with tennis courts and swimming pools. As well as the domestic bungalow, all tea estates had an office bungalow where the owners could deal with the mountains of bureaucratic paperwork that came with the job. The planters who were at the top of their profession tended to live in and around the town of Newara Eliya, a kind of mini-Britain, with Victorian architecture that would have looked equally at home in an English village or a Scottish glen.

The town became an even more attractive destination, especially for women, when the railroad was built, making it much less cut-off from the rest of the country. With the train came European-style shops selling groceries and fabrics, and then a strong social network developed among the European community, which included drinking and dinner clubs, horse-racing, polo, golf, and even fox-hunting clubs. Back in Victorian Britain, Ceylon, as Sri Lanka was then known, became a hot topic of conversation among the chattering classes, who were already in the swing of the new ritual of "Tea and Sandwiches." Ceylon tea, with its distinctive island flavor, became a must-have commodity in certain social circles!

Today, after the land reform act of 1971 that quite rightly required land to be given back to Sri Lankan ownership, most tea plantations are now Sri Lankan–owned. Mr. P. R. Perera, a Sri Lankan, manages the Hethersett Tea Factory.

The entrance to Flowerdew Cottage Garden.

Skill level: Intermediate.

Size: Approximately 24" (61cm) diameter.

Materials:

3 balls Rowan Cotton Glace, 100% cotton [1¾ oz (50g), 137yds (115m)], Bleached. **2** fine
24 glass beads, approximately ½" (13mm) long.
Size 8 (5mm) set of 5 double-pointed needles and 16" (40.5cm) circular needle.

Note: Begin on double-pointed needles, change to circular needle when you have too many stitches
to work comfortably on the double-points.

Cast on 8 stitches to the double-pointed needles, divide evenly between 4 of them and join into a round. Mark the join.

Rounds 1 and 2: Knit.

Round 3: *Yo, k1, repeat from * around.

Round 4 (and every alternate round): Knit.

Round 5: *Yo, k2, repeat around.

Round 7: *Yo, k3, repeat around. 32 stitches.

Round 9: *Yo, k1, yo, sl1, k1, psso, k1, repeat from * around.

Round 11: *Yo, k1, yo, sl1, k1, psso, k2, repeat from * around.

Round 13: *Yo, k1, yo, sl1, k1, psso, k3, repeat from * around. 56 stitches.

Round 15: *Yo, k1, (yo, sl1, k1, psso) twice, k2, repeat from * around.

Round 17: *Yo, k1, (yo, sl1, k1, psso) twice, k3, repeat from * around.

Round 19: *Yo, k1, (yo, sl1, k1, psso) 3 times, k2, repeat from * around.

Round 21: *Yo, k1, (yo, sl1, k1, psso) 3 times, k3, repeat from * around.

Round 23: *Yo, k1, (yo, sl1, k1, psso) 3 times, k4, repeat from * around.

Round 25: *Yo, k1, (yo, sl1, k1, psso) 3 times, k5, repeat from * around.

Round 27: *Yo, k1, (yo, sl1, k1, psso) 3 times, k6, repeat from * around.

Round 29: *Yo, k1, (yo, sl1, k1, psso) 3 times, k7, repeat from * around. 120 stitches.

Round 31: *Yo, k1, (yo, sl1, k1, psso) 3 times, k1, sl1, k1, psso (yo) twice, sl1, k1, psso, k3, repeat from * around.

Round 32 (and every alternate round): Knit, working (k1, p1) into every (yo) twice from the previous round.

Round 33: *Yo, k1, (yo, sl1, k1, psso) 3 times, k2, sl1, k1, psso, (yo) twice, sl1, k1, psso, k3, repeat from * around.

Round 35: *Yo, k1, (yo, sl1, k1, psso) 3 times, k1, sl1, k1, psso, yo, k3, sl1, k1, psso, yo, k2, repeat from * around.

Round 37: *Yo, k1, (yo, sl1, k1, psso) 3 times, sl1, k1, psso, (yo) twice, sl1, k1, psso, k4, (yo) twice, sl1, k1, psso, k1, repeat from * around.

Round 39: *Yo, k1, (yo, sl1, k1, psso) 3 times, k3, (yo) twice, k3tog, k1, k3tog, (yo) twice, sl1, k1, psso, k1, repeat from * around.

Round 41: *Yo, k1, (yo, sl1, k1, psso) 3 times, k3, sl1, k1, psso, (yo) 3 times, k5tog, (yo) 3 times, sl1, k1, psso, k1, repeat from * around.

Round 42 (and every alternate round): Knit, working (k1, p1, k1) into any (yo) 3 times from the previous round, and (k1, p1) into any (yo) twice.

Round 43: *Yo, k1, (yo, sl1, k1, psso) 3 times, k3, (yo) twice, k4, sl1, k1, psso, (yo) twice, k5, repeat from * around.

Round 45: *Yo, k1, (yo, sl1, k1, psso) 3 times, k5, (yo) twice, k3tog, k1, k3tog, (yo) twice, sl1, k1, psso, k4, repeat from * around.

Round 47: *Yo, k1, (yo, sl1, k1, psso) 3 times, k4, k3tog, (yo) 3 times, k5tog, (yo) 3 times, k3tog, k3, repeat from * around. 192 stitches.

Round 49: *Yo, k1, (yo, sl1, k1, psso) 3 times, k2, sl1, k1, psso, (yo) twice, k4, sl1, k1, psso, (yo) twice, k3, sl1, k1, psso, k2, repeat from * around.

Round 51: *Yo, k1, (yo, sl1, k1, psso) 3 times, k5, [(yo) twice, k3tog, k1, k3tog] twice, repeat from * around.

Round 53: *Yo, k1, (yo, sl, k1, psso) 3 times, k5, sl1, k1, psso, (yo) 3 times, k5tog, (yo) 3 times, sl1, k1, psso, k2, repeat from * around. 192 stitches.

Rounds 54–56: Knit.

Round 57: *K7, yo, k1, yo, repeat from * around.

Round 58: *Sl1, k1, psso, k3, k2tog, yo, k3, yo repeat from * around.

Round 59: *Sl1, k1, psso, k1, k2tog, yo, k5, yo repeat from * around.

Round 60: *K3tog, yo, k3, yo, sl1, k1, psso, k2, yo, repeat from * around.

Round 61: *K1, yo, sl1, k1, psso, k5, k2tog, yo, repeat from * around.

Round 62: K2 * yo, sl1, k1, psso, k3, k2tog, yo, k3, repeat from * to the last stitch, k1.

Round 63: K3 *yo, sl1, k1, psso, k1, k2tog, yo, k5, repeat from * to the last 2 stitches, k2.

Round 64: Knit.

Round 65: K4, *sl1, k2tog, psso, k7, turn, sl1, p2, make 7 by working (k1, p1) 3 times and k1 once again into the next stitch, p4, sl1, turn, bind off 14 stitches, repeat from * around. Fasten off securely.

Dampen tablecloth and block out, pinning each point for the best effect. Sew a bead onto each point when the tablecloth has dried.

GIRL'S ARGYLE CARDIGAN

GIRL'S ARGYLE CARDIGAN

Skill level: Intermediate.

Size: Age 2(4, 6, 8) years [S(M, L, XL)].

Finished chest: 26(28, 30, 32)".

Materials:

8(9, 10, 10) balls RYC Baby Alpaca DK, 100% Alpaca [1¾ oz (50g), 109yd (100m)], 4(5, 6, 6) Chambray, 2(2, 2, 2) each in Blossom and Thistle. **(3)** light

Approximately 1,650(1,800, 1,950, 2,100) 4mm pearlescent white glass beads.

7 buttons.

Size 3 and 6 (3.25 and 4mm) needles.

Gauge: 20 stitches and 27 rows to 4" (10cm) on size 6 (4mm) needles over stockinette stitch intarsia Argyle pattern.

Back

Cast on 65(71, 75, 81) stitches using 3 (3.25mm) needles and Chambray. Work 2(2, 2, 2½)" (5[5, 5, 6]cm) in k1, p1 rib. Thread beads onto all 3 colors of yarn. Change to size 6 (4mm) needles and work Argyle and bead pattern in intarsia from chart, placing beads where indicated until the back measures 8½ (9¼, 9¾, 10¼)" (21.5[23.5, 25, 26]cm) from the cast-on edge, ending with the right side facing for the next row. For the smaller sizes, do not place beads on the edge stitches of the back, as this will make sewing up difficult. Shape armholes:

Next row: Bind off 2(2, 3, 3) stitches at the beginning of the next 2 rows, then 1 stitch at the beginning of the next 4(4, 6, 8) right-side rows. 57(63, 63, 67) stitches. Work even until armhole measures 5(5¼, 5¾, 6¼)" (13[13.5, 14.5, 16]cm). Shape shoulders:

Small, Medium, and Large: Bind off 7(8, 8) stitches at the beginning of the next 4 rows, place the remaining 29(31, 31) stitches onto a holder for the back neck.

X-Large: Bind off 9 stitches at the beginning of the next 2 rows, then 8 stitches at the beginning of the following 2 rows. Place the remaining 33 stitches onto a holder for the back neck.

Left front

Cast on 36(39, 41, 44) stitches using size 3 (3.25mm) needles and Chambray. Work 2(2, 2, 2½)" (5[5, 5, 6]cm) in k1, p1 rib. Change to size 6 (4mm) needles, and work in Argyle and bead pattern in intarsia from chart, work 30(33, 35, 38) stitches. Leave remaining 6 stitches on a holder for front button band. Work even until the front measures 8½ (9¼, 9¾, 10¼)" (21.5[23.5, 25, 26]cm) from the cast-on edge with the right side facing for the next row. Shape armhole:

Next row: Bind off 2(2, 3, 3) stitches at the beginning of the row, then 1 stitch at the beginning of the next 2(2, 3, 4) right-side rows. 26(29, 29, 31) stitches. Work even until the armhole measures 2½(2½, 2¾, 2¾)" (6[6, 7, 7]cm), ending with the wrong side facing to begin neck shaping.

Small: Bind off 3, 3, 3, 2, 1 stitches at the beginning of the next 5 wrong-side rows. Work even until the armhole measures 5" (13cm), shape shoulders by binding off 7 stitches on the next 2 right-side rows.

Medium and Large: Bind off 3, 3, 3, 2, 1, 1 stitches at the beginning of the next 6 wrong-side rows, work even until the armhole measures 5¼(5¾)" ([13.5, 14.5]cm), shape shoulders by binding off 8 stitches on the next 2 right-side rows.

X-Large: Bind off 3, 3, 3, 2, 1, 1, 1 stitches at the beginning of the next 7 wrong-side rows, work even until the armhole measures 6¼" (16cm), shape shoulders by binding off 9 stitches at the beginning of the next right-side row, then the remaining 8 stitches on the next right-side row.

Right front

Cast on 36(39, 41, 44) stitches using size 3 (3.25mm) needles and Chambray. Work 4(4, 4, 6) rows k1, p1 rib. Place 1st buttonhole on 5th (5th, 5th, 7th) row—rib 4, yo, k2tog. Continue until ribbing measures 2(2, 2, 2½)" (5[5, 5, 6]cm), with the right side of work facing. Do not break yarn. Slip first 6 stitches onto holder for buttonhole band, rejoin new yarn (with beads threaded) to the remaining stitches, change to size 6 (4mm) needles and work Argyle and bead pattern in intarsia from chart. Work even until the front measures 8½ (9¼, 9¾, 10¼)" (21.5[23.5, 25, 26]cm) from the cast-on edge with the wrong side facing for the next row. Shape armhole:

Next row: Bind off 2(2, 3, 3) stitches at the beginning of the row, then 1 stitch at the beginning of the next 2(2, 3, 4) wrong-side rows. 26(29, 29, 31) stitches. Work

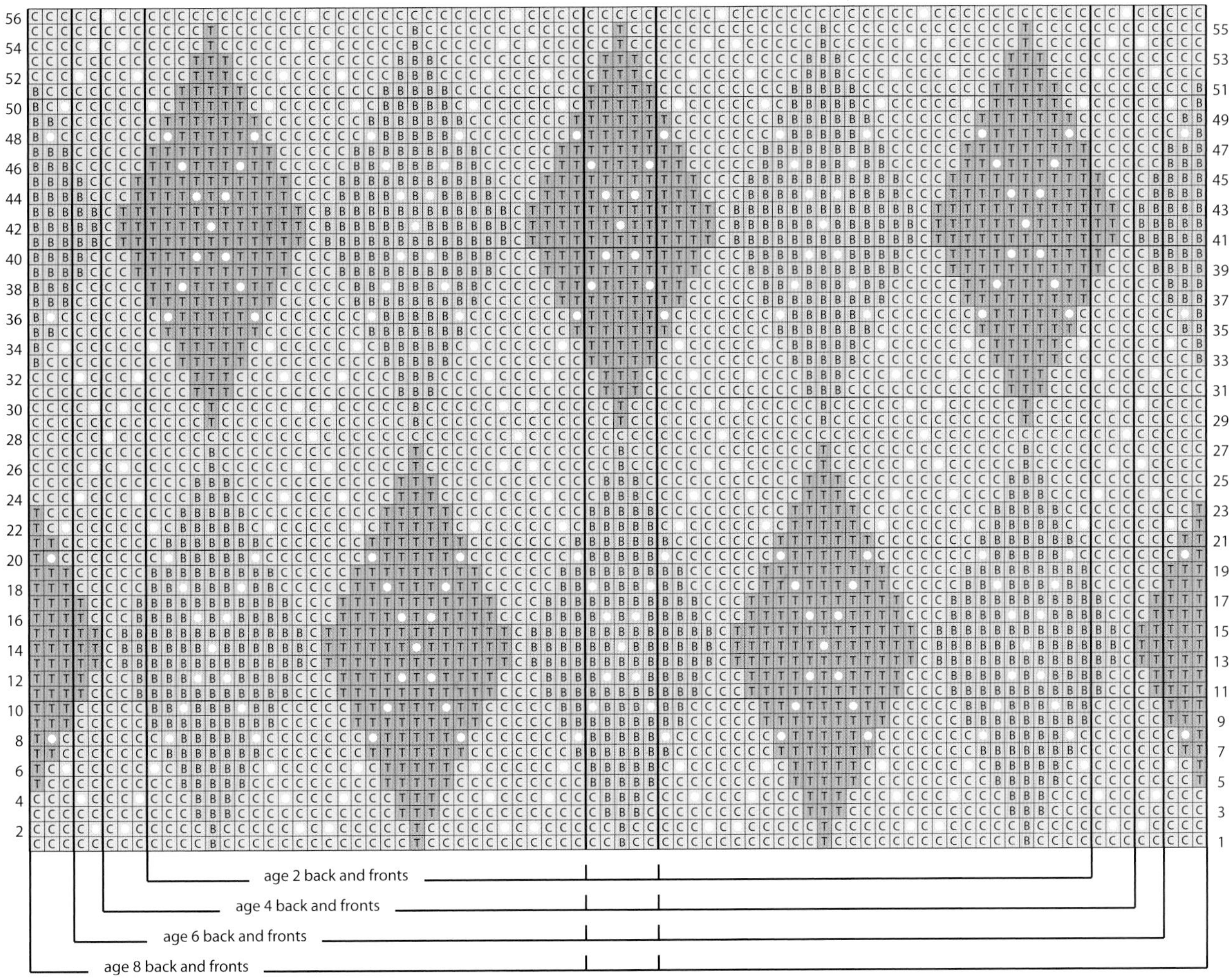

age 2 back and fronts

age 4 back and fronts

age 6 back and fronts

age 8 back and fronts

C Chambray stitch. Knit on right side, purl on wrong side.

☐ Chambray stitch with bead. Knit to this stitch, bring yarn forward, push bead up to the front of the work, slip this stitch purlwise, take yarn back, knit the next stitch as usual.

B Blossom stitch. Knit on right side, purl on wrong side.

☐ Blossom stitch with bead. Knit to this stitch, bring yarn forward, push bead up to the front of the work, slip this stitch purlwise, take yarn back, knit the next stitch as usual.

T Thistle stitch. Knit on right side, purl on wrong side.

☐ Thistle Stitch with bead. Knit to this stitch, bring yarn forward, push bead up to the front of the work, slip this stitch purlwise, take yarn back, knit the next stitch as usual.

age 2 sleeve
age 4 sleeve
age 6 sleeve
age 8 sleeve

C — Chambray stitch. Knit on right side, purl on wrong side.

Chambray stitch with bead. Knit to this stitch, bring yarn forward, push bead up to the front of the work, slip this stitch purlwise, take yarn back, knit the next stitch as usual.

B — Blossom stitch. Knit on right side, purl on wrong side.

Blossom stitch with bead. Knit to this stitch, bring yarn forward, push bead up to the front of the work, slip this stitch purlwise, take yarn back, knit the next stitch as usual.

T — Thistle stitch. Knit on right side, purl on wrong side.

Thistle Stitch with bead. Knit to this stitch, bring yarn forward, push bead up to the front of the work, slip this stitch purlwise, take yarn back, knit the next stitch as usual.

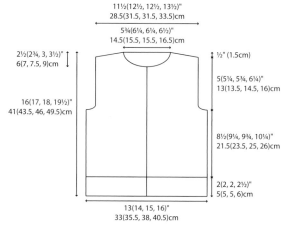

11½(12½, 12½, 13½)"
28.5(31.5, 31.5, 33.5)cm

5¾(6¼, 6¼, 6½)"
14.5(15.5, 15.5, 16.5)cm

2½(2¾, 3, 3½)"
6(7, 7.5, 9)cm

½" (1.5cm)

5(5¼, 5¾, 6¼)"
13(13.5, 14.5, 16)cm

16(17, 18, 19½)"
41(43.5, 46, 49.5)cm

8½(9¼, 9¾, 10¼)"
21.5(23.5, 25, 26)cm

2(2, 2, 2½)"
5(5, 5, 6)cm

13(14, 15, 16)"
33(35.5, 38, 40.5)cm

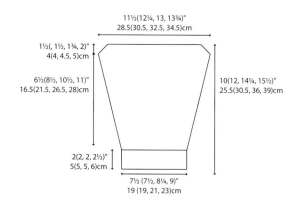

11½(12¼, 13, 13¾)"
28.5(30.5, 32.5, 34.5)cm

1½(, 1½, 1¾, 2)"
4(4, 4.5, 5)cm

6½(8½, 10½, 11)"
16.5(21.5, 26.5, 28)cm

10(12, 14¼, 15½)"
25.5(30.5, 36, 39)cm

2(2, 2, 2½)"
5(5, 5, 6)cm

7½ (7½, 8¼, 9)"
19 (19, 21, 23)cm

even until the armhole measures 2½(2½, 2¾, 2¾)" (6[6, 7, 7]cm), ending with the right side facing to begin neck shaping.

Small: Bind off 3, 3, 3, 2, 1 stitches at the beginning of the next 5 right-side rows. Work even until the armhole measures 5" (13cm), shape shoulders by binding off 7 stitches on the next 2 wrong-side rows.

Medium and Large: Bind off 3, 3, 3, 2, 1, 1 stitches at the beginning of the next 6 right-side rows. Work even until the armhole measures 5¼(5¾)" (13.5, [14.5]cm), shape shoulders by binding off 8 stitches on the next 2 wrong-side rows.

X-Large: Bind off 3, 3, 3, 2, 1, 1, 1 stitches at the beginning of the next 7 right-side rows, work even until the armhole measures 6¼" (16cm), shape shoulders by binding off 9 stitches at the beginning of the next wrong-side row, then the remaining 8 stitches on the following wrong-side row.

Sleeves

Cast on 37(37, 41, 45) stitches using size 3 (3.25mm) needles. Work 2(2, 2, 2½)" (5[5, 5, 6]cm) in k1, p1 rib. Thread beads onto all 3 colors of yarn. Change to size 6 (4mm) needles, and work in Argyle and bead pattern from chart for size as indicated. Increase 1 stitch (k1, m1, k to last stitch, m1, k1) at each end of the 5th(5th, 3rd, 3rd) and every following 4th(4th, 6th, 6th) row until there are 57(61, 65, 69) stitches, work even until the sleeve measures 8½(10½, 12½, 13½)" (21.5[26.5, 32, 34]cm) from cast-on edge, with the right side facing for the next row. Shape sleeve top:

Next row: Bind off 2(2, 3, 3) stitches at the beginning of the next 2 rows, then 1 stitch at the beginning of the next 8(8, 10, 12) right-side rows. Bind off remaining stitches.

Button band

Rejoin Chambray yarn to stitches on the left front at the inside edge. M1, rib to end. 7 stitches. Work in k1, p1 rib, but keeping the made stitch in stockinette stitch (for ease of sewing band to the front) until the band reaches to the neck edge when slightly stretched. Mark 5 button placements evenly up the band—final (7th) buttonhole will be worked in the neckband.

Buttonhole band

With the right side of the front facing, slip stitches back onto size 3 (3.25mm) needles, join in Chambray yarn, rib across the 5 stitches, kfb. 7 stitches. Work in k1, p1 rib, again keeping the made stitch in stockinette stitch, working buttonholes to match button placements as marked on the button band. Work these buttonholes rib 3, yo, k2tog. Work until the buttonhole band reaches the front neck when slightly stretched.

Neckband

Join shoulder seams. Rib across the first 5 stitches of the right front buttonhole band, k2tog, pick up 23(25, 27, 31) stitches up the right front neck, knit across the 29(29, 31, 33) stitches held for the back neck, pick up and knit 23(25, 27, 31) stitches down the left-front neck, knit the first 2 stitches from the button band together, rib the last 5 stitches. 85(89, 95, 105) stitches. Work 1 row rib, place buttonhole on the next row, (rib 3, yo, k2tog, rib to end of row). Work a further 5 rows ribbing, bind off in rib.

Finishing

Sew sleeves into armholes. Join side and sleeve seams, sew on buttons. Sew in ends.

Fruitcake

FROM THE TEA FACTORY

Traditional fruitcake recipes were brought over to Sri Lanka by the British wives of the tea planters in the nineteenth and twentieth centuries.

Makes one 8-inch (20.5cm) cake; serves 15

2 sticks (225 grams) unsalted butter, softened

1¼ cup (250 grams) sugar

8 large eggs, beaten

1¾ cup (250 grams) all-purpose flour

⅓ cup (45 grams) cornstarch

1 teaspoon (5 grams) baking powder

2 cups (240 grams) mixed dried fruit

Preheat the oven to 325°F (160°C). Grease an 8-inch (20.3cm) round cake pan with sides at least 3 inches (7.5cm) high.

Beat the butter and sugar in an electric mixer until creamy in texture. Gradually add in the beaten eggs.

In a separate bowl, mix together the flour, cornstarch, and baking powder. Slowly mix the dry ingredients into the beaten egg mixture. Fold in the dried fruit.

Pour the mixture into the prepared pan. Bake for one hour and 10 minutes, until a metal skewer inserted in the center comes out dry.

Cool on a wire rack before unmolding.

The Tea Factory

Kandapola
Nuwara Eliya
Sri Lanka

tfactory@slt.lk

The Tea Factory is situated 6,850 feet (2,088 meters) above sea level and is a traditional tea factory that has been converted into an award-winning hotel. If you stay on the fourth floor, you are sleeping at the highest elevation in Sri Lanka! There is still a working tea factory on the premises and you can go out and pluck your own tea, which the factory will then process and package for you as part of your stay.

The views are panoramic over the tea plantations, many of them with Scottish and English names. The climate is much colder than in the rest of Sri Lanka, so at most times of year, you will need to take knitwear. The teas are delicious as is the rest of the cooking; you can choose between traditional Sri Lankan fare and British favorites brought from the recipe books of the early planters' wives.

THE PROCESSING OF TEA

Tea is processed using the following steps:

Withering
The young shoots of the tea plant are dried on racks on the upper stories of the tea factory, where currents of air from the open windows flow through the racks.

Rolling
A roller squeezes out the juices that give the tea its characteristic flavor. The rolling also gives the leaf its twisted or curled shape.

Fermentation
After rolling, the leaves are laid out on glass or cement tables in a cool, humid atmosphere. Here, oxidization takes place, and the color of the leaves changes from green to a coppery shade.

Drying or Firing
This takes place in a large chamber fitted with trays that rotate while hot air heated by a furnace is forced into the chamber. This stops the oxidization process and changes the color of the leaves once again to black.

Sorting
This occurs when the leaves are graded by size and packed into tea chests or foil sacks.

Shipping
The tea packed in chests or sacks makes its way to the capital city of Colombo, which houses the largest tea auction center in the world. It is then loaded onto ships for its long journey to tea-drinking countries around the globe.

Tasting
Quite an art, like wine tasting, this takes years of experience to learn.

chapter two

SOMERSET SINGLE ESTATE TEA

To the west of Newara Eliya, Sri Lanka, on the road to Hatton, lies the tiny village of Radella in the misty Dimbula Valley. Here you come across the signpost to the Dimbula Cricket ground, which was created by the British tea planters in 1873 and has been used for cricket ever since. Cricket is synonymous with tea in both the United Kingdom and Sri Lanka, the two countries being absolutely passionate for the sport and the drink in equal measure. Whether you are watching a cricket match on a sleepy village green in England or on a pitch in a clearing in a jungle village in Sri Lanka, both games will "stop for tea."

In the hot summer months, as well as the usual sandwiches and cakes served at teatime in cricket pavilions, cricket clubs often provide "Strawberry Teas." These consist of a fine-brewed tea such as Somerset Single Estate, which has an exotic, slightly fruity flavor and a deep amber hue.

Dimbula Cricket Ground.

The tea is accompanied by a bowl of fresh strawberries and ice cream or cream. The Dimbula Athletic & Cricket Club is fortunate to have the "Somerset Tea Boutique" at the end of the road, which is part of the Somerset Tea Estate. Here, cricketers and fans can enjoy a "Strawberry Tea," in which strawberries and ice cream are served with a topping of homemade strawberry jam particular to this establishment.

The game of cricket has always had its own special knitwear as part of the overall uniform. Cricket attire is known as "cricket whites." Traditionally, one only wears white or cream, although modern cricket clothing now features some much brighter colors. The classic cricket sweaters are usually cabled and striped with the club colors in bandings around the V-neck, cuffs, and waistband. The same colorations also apply to cricket slipovers (vests), which are the sleeveless versions of the sweaters. Cricket blazers are woven with club colors either in a stripe or with colored piping, and they often have their breast pockets monogrammed with the club insignia. We had fun turning these traditional blazers into a knit!

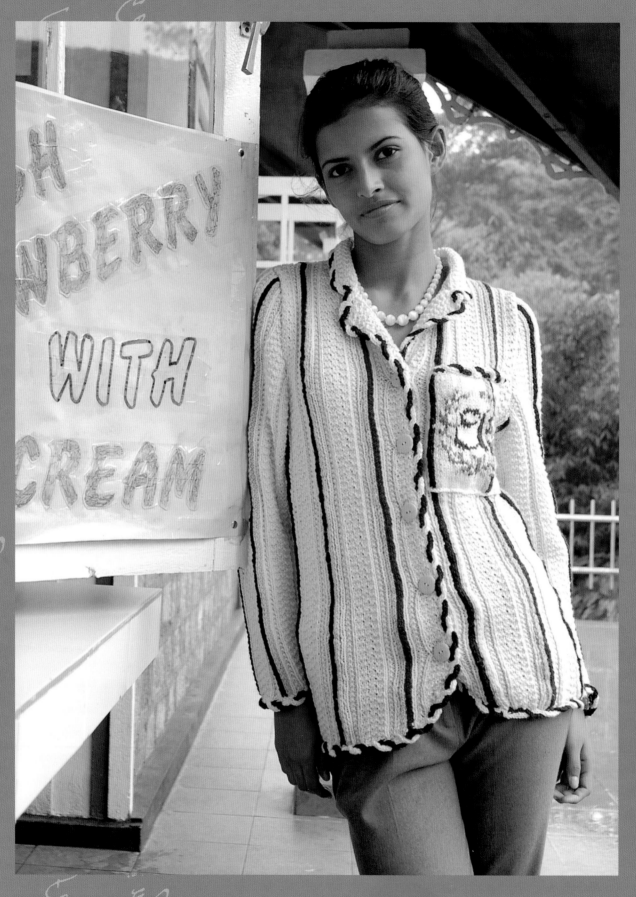

Skill level: Intermediate.

Size: XS (S, M, L, XL, XXL).

Finished bust: 34(36½, 41, 45, 49, 53)" (86[93, 104, 114, 124.5, 134.5]cm).

Materials:
18(18, 19, 20, 21, 22) balls RYC Cashsoft DK, 57% Extra Fine Merino Wool, 33% Microfiber, 10% Cashmere (3) light
[1¾ oz (50g), 142yd (130m)], 10(10, 11, 12, 13, 14) Cream, 2 each of Sweet, Poison, and Navy, 1 each of Lichen and Lime.
Size 6 (4mm) and 5 (3.75mm) needles.

Gauge: 23 stitches and 32 rows to 4"(10cm) over texture and stripe pattern on size 6 (4mm) needles. Note: Row gauge is important in this pattern, otherwise the front neck shaping will not work out correctly.

Back

Cast on 104(110, 124, 136, 150, 162) stitches using Cream and size 6 (4mm) needles. Working from texture stitch chart appropriate for the size you are knitting, work as follows (the stripes should be worked using the intarsia method with the yarns twisted together to avoid holes, but the background color should be carried across the back of the stripes as for Fair Isle knitting):

X-Small: 20 stitches in texture pattern, 2 Poison, 2 Sweet, 16 texture, repeat from *, ending with 20 stitches in texture pattern.

Small: 3 stitches in texture pattern, * 2 Sweet, 2 Navy, 16 texture, 2 Poison, 2 Sweet, 16 texture, repeat from *, ending with 3 stitches of texture pattern.

Medium: 10 stitches in texture pattern, * 2 Sweet, 2 Navy, 16 texture pattern, 2 Poison, 2 Sweet, 16 texture, repeat from *, ending with 10 stitches of wave pattern.

Large: 16 stitches in texture pattern, * 2 Sweet, 2 in Navy, 16 texture pattern, 2 Poison, 2 Sweet, 16 texture pattern, repeat from *.

X-Large: 3 stitches in texture pattern, * 2 Poison, 2 Sweet, 16 texture, 2 Sweet, 2 Navy, 16 texture pattern, repeat from *, ending with 3 stitches of wave pattern.

XX-Large: 9 stitches in texture pattern, * 2 Poison, 2 Sweet, 16 texture, 2 Sweet, 2 in Navy, 16 of texture pattern, repeat from *, ending with 9 stitches of wave pattern.

Work straight for 2 (2, 2, 2, 2½, 2½)" (5[5, 5, 5, 6.5, 6.5]cm). Begin decreases:

Next row: Decrease 1 stitch at each end of the row (sl1, k1, psso, work in pattern to the last 2 stitches, k2tog), then repeat this row three times more at 2" (5cm) intervals. 96(102, 116, 128, 142, 154) stitches. Work even for 2½(2½, 2¾, 2¾, 2¾, 2¾)" (6.5[6.5, 7, 7, 7, 7]cm), ending with the right side facing for the next row.

Next row (increase): Increase 1 stitch at each end of the next row, work even for

2½" (6.5cm) (all sizes), work increase row again. 100(106, 120, 132, 146, 160) stitches. Work even until the back measures 15¾(16½, 17, 17¼, 17¼, 17¾)" (40[42, 43, 44, 44, 45]cm) from the cast-on edge.

Shape armholes

Keeping the pattern correct, bind off:

X-Small: 3 stitches at the beginning of the next 4 rows, then 2 on the next 2 rows. Decrease 1 stitch at each end of the next row. 82 stitches. Work even until the armhole measures 8" (20.5cm).

Small: 4 stitches at the beginning of the next 2 rows, then 3 on the next 2 rows, 2 on the next 2 rows. Decrease 1 stitch at each end of the next row. 86 stitches. Work even until the armhole measures 8¼" (21cm).

Medium: 4 stitches at the beginning of the next 2 rows, then 3 on the next 2 rows, then 2 on the next 4 rows. Decrease 1 stitch at each end of the next 6 right-side rows. 86 stitches. Work even until the armhole measures 8¼" (21cm).

Large: 4 stitches at the beginning of the next 4 rows, then 3 on the next 4 rows, then 2 on the next 4 rows. Decrease 1 stitch at each end of the next 3 right-side rows. 90 stitches. Work even until the armhole measures 8½" (22cm).

X-Large: 5 stitches at the beginning of the next 2 rows, then 4 on the next 4 rows, then 3 on the next 6 rows, and 2 on the next 4 rows. Decrease 1 stitch at each end of the next 2 right-side rows. 90 stitches. Work even until the armhole measures 8½" (22cm).

XX-Large: 5 stitches on the next 2 rows, then 4 on the next 6 rows, 3 on the next 6 rows, and 2 on the next 4 rows. Decrease 1 stitch at each end of the next 2 right-side rows. 94 stitches. Work even until the armhole measures 9" (23cm).

Shape shoulders and back neck

Bind off 3(4, 3, 4, 4, 4) stitches at the beginning of the next 2 rows, 4(4, 4, 4, 4, 4) stitches at the beginning of the following 4 rows.

*__Next row:__ Bind off 4(4, 4, 4, 4, 5), pattern 9(9, 9, 10, 10, 10), [10(10, 10, 11, 11, 11) stitches on right-hand needle], turn.

__Next row:__ p2tog, work in pattern to end.

__Next row:__ Bind off 4(4, 4, 5, 5, 5), work in pattern to the last 2 stitches, k2tog.

__Next row:__ work in pattern to end.

__Next row:__ Bind off the remaining stitches.

Rejoin yarn to the remaining stitches, bind off the central 32(32, 34, 34, 34, 36) stitches for the back neck, work in pattern to end. Work from * to complete the left shoulder.

Left front

Cast on 39(42, 49, 55, 62, 68) stitches using Cream and size 6 (4mm) needles. Working from texture stitch chart appropriate for the size you are knitting, work:

__X-Small:__ 20 stitches in texture pattern, 2 Poison, 2 Sweet, 15 stitches in texture pattern.

__Small:__ 3 stitches in texture pattern, 2 Sweet, 2 Navy, 16 stitches in texture pattern, 2 Poison, 2 Sweet, 15 stitches in texture pattern.

__Medium:__ 10 stitches in texture pattern, 2 Sweet, 2 Navy, 16 stitches in texture pattern, 2 Poison, 2 Sweet, 15 stitches in texture pattern.

__Large:__ 16 stitches in texture pattern, 2 Sweet, 2 Navy, 16 stitches in texture pattern, 2 Poison, 2 Sweet, 15 stitches in texture pattern.

__X-Large:__ 3 stitches texture pattern, 2 Poison, 2 Sweet, 16 stitches in texture pattern, 2 Sweet, 2 Navy, 16 stitches in texture pattern, 2 Poison, 2 Sweet, 15 stitches in texture pattern.

__XX-Large:__ 9 stitches in texture pattern, 2 Poison, 2 Sweet, 16 stitches in texture pattern, 2 Sweet, 2 Navy, 16 stitches in texture pattern, 2 Poison, 2 Sweet, 15 stitches in texture pattern.

Working in pattern as set, cast on 3, 2, 2, stitches on the next and 2 following wrong-side rows (center front of Blazer), then 1 stitch on every following row (right side and wrong side) 5 times, then on every wrong-side row twice, then on every other wrong-side row twice, taking increased stitches into stripe and texture pattern. 55(58, 65, 71, 78, 84) stitches. You should end on the 11th stitch of the texture pattern and have another set of Sweet and Navy stripes, as on the Back.

Decrease 1 stitch at the side edge (beginning of right-side rows) when the front measures 2(2, 2, 2, 2½, 2½)" (5[5, 5, 5, 6.5, 6.5]cm), then repeat this decrease row three times more at 2" (5cm) intervals. 51(54, 61, 67, 74, 80) stitches. Work even for 2½(2½, 2¾, 2¾, 2¾, 2¾)" (6.5[6.5, 7, 7, 7, 7]cm), ending with the right side facing for the next row.

__Next row (increase):__ Increase 1 stitch at the side edge of the next row, work even for 2½" (6.5cm) (all sizes), work increase row again. 53(56, 63, 69, 76, 82) stitches. Work even until the back measures 15¾(16½, 17, 17¼, 17¼, 17¾)" (40[42, 43, 44, 44, 45]cm) from the cast-on edge. Shape armholes, keeping pattern correct bind off:

__X-Small:__ 3 stitches at the beginning of the next 2 right-side rows, then 2 on the next right-side rows. Decrease 1 stitch at the beginning of the next right-side row. AT THE SAME TIME, when front measures 18½" (47cm) from the cast-on edge with the wrong side facing, shape the front neck:

Decrease 1 stitch at the neck edge on the next and every following 3rd row until armhole measures 8" (20.5cm), when shoulder shaping begins. At the same time as continuing to decrease on every 3rd row at neck edge, bind off 3 stitches at beginning of next RS row for shoulder, then 4 stitches at the beginning of next 5 right-side rows.

__Small:__ 4 stitches at the beginning of the next right-side row, then 3 on the next right-side row, and 2 on the next right-side row. Decrease 1 stitch at the beginning of the next right-side row. AT THE SAME TIME, when front measures 18½" (47cm) from the cast-on edge with the wrong side facing, shape the front neck:

Decrease 1 stitch at the neck edge on the next and every following 3rd row until armhole measures 8¼" (21cm), when shoulder shaping begins. AT THE SAME TIME as continuing to decrease on every 3rd row at neck edge, bind off 4 stitches at the beginning of the next right-side row for shoulder, then 4 stitches at beginning of next 3 RS rows, work even at the neck edge from now on, bind off 4 stitches on the next right-side row and the remaining 5 stitches on the next right side.

__Medium:__ 4 stitches at the beginning of the right-side row, then 3 on the next right side-row, then 2 on the next 2 right-side rows. Decrease 1 stitch at the beginning of the next 3 right-side rows. AT THE SAME TIME, when front measures 18½" (47cm) from the cast-on edge with the wrong side facing, shape the front neck: Decrease 1 stitch at the neck edge on the next and every following 3rd row until armhole measures 8¼" (21cm), when shoulder shaping begins. AT THE SAME TIME

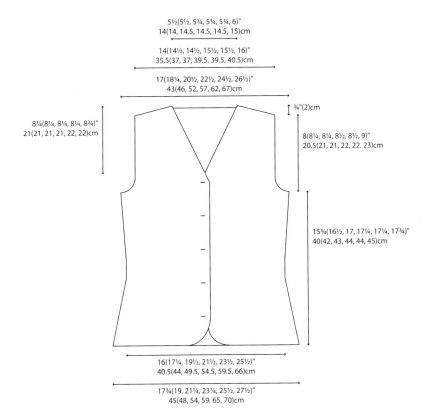

5½(5½, 5¾, 5¾, 5¾, 6)"
14(14, 14.5, 14.5, 14.5, 15)cm

14(14½, 14½, 15½, 15½, 16)"
35.5(37, 37, 39.5, 39.5, 40.5)cm

17(18¼, 20½, 22½, 24½, 26½)"
43(46, 52, 57, 62, 67)cm

8¼(8¼, 8¼, 8¼, 8¾)"
21(21, 21, 21, 22, 22)cm

¾"(2)cm

8(8¼, 8¼, 8½, 8½, 9)"
20.5(21, 21, 22, 22, 23)cm

15¾(16½, 17, 17¼, 17¼, 17¾)"
40(42, 43, 44, 44, 45)cm

16(17¼, 19½, 21½, 23½, 25½)"
40.5(44, 49.5, 54.5, 59.5, 66)cm

17¾(19, 21¼, 23¼, 25½, 27½)"
45(48, 54, 59, 65, 70)cm

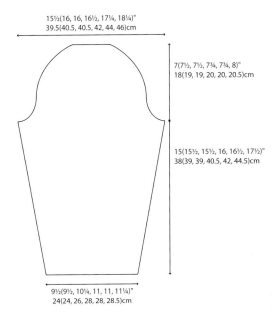

15½(16, 16½, 17¼, 18¼)"
39.5(40.5, 40.5, 42, 44, 46)cm

7(7½, 7½, 7¾, 7¾, 8)"
18(19, 19, 20, 20, 20.5)cm

15(15½, 15½, 16, 16½, 17½)"
38(39, 39, 40.5, 42, 44.5)cm

9½(9½, 10¼, 11, 11, 11¼)"
24(24, 26, 28, 28, 28.5)cm

as continuing to decrease on every 3rd row at neck edge, bind off 3 stitches at the beginning of the next right-side row for shoulder, then 4 stitches at the beginning of the next 5 RS rows.

Large: 4 stitches at the beginning of the next 2 right-side rows, then 3 on the next 2 right-side rows, then 2 on the next 2 right-side rows. Decrease 1 stitch at the beginning of the next 3 right-side rows. AT THE SAME TIME, when front measures 18½" (47cm) from the cast-on edge with the wrong side facing, shape the front neck:
Decrease 1 stitch at the neck edge on the next and every following 3rd row until armhole measures 8½" (22cm), when shoulder shaping begins. AT THE SAME TIME as continuing to decrease on every 3rd row at neck edge, bind off 4 stitches at the beginning of the next 4 right-side rows for shoulder, work even at the neck edge from now on, bind off 5 stitches at the beginning of the next 2 right-side rows.

X-Large: 5 stitches at the beginning of the next right-side row, then 4 on the next 2 right-side rows, then 3 on the next 3 right-side rows, and 2 on the next 2 right-side rows. Decrease 1 stitch at the beginning of the next right-side row. AT THE SAME

TIME, when front measures 18½" (47cm) from the cast-on edge with the wrong side facing, shape the front neck:
Decrease 1 stitch at the neck edge on the next and every following 3rd row until armhole measures 8½" (22cm), when shoulder shaping begins. At the same time as continuing to decrease on every 3rd row at neck edge, bind off 4 stitches at the beginning of the next 4 right-side rows for shoulder, work even at the neck edge from now on, bind off 5 stitches at the beginning of the next 2 right-side rows.

XX-Large: 5 stitches on the next right-side row, then 4 on the next 3 right-side rows, 3 on the next 3 right-side rows, and 2 on the next 2 right-side rows. Decrease 1 stitch at the beginning of the next 2 right-side rows. AT THE SAME TIME, when front measures 18½" (47cm) from the cast-on edge with the wrong side facing, shape the front neck:
Decrease 1 stitch at the neck edge on the next and every following 3rd row until armhole measures 9" (23cm), when shoulder shaping begins. At the same time as continuing to decrease on every 3rd row at neck edge, bind off 4 stitches at the beginning of the next 3 right-side rows for shoulder, work even at the neck edge from now on, bind off 5 stitches at the beginning of the next 3 right-side rows.

Right front

Cast on 39(42, 49, 55, 62, 68) stitches using Cream and size 6 (4mm) needles.

Beginning from stitch 2 on the texture chart for all sizes, work:

X-Small: 15 stitches in texture pattern, 2 Sweet, 2 Navy, 20 stitches in texture pattern.

Small: 15 stitches in texture pattern, 2 Sweet, 2 Navy, 16 stitches in texture pattern, 2 Poison, 2 Sweet, 3 stitches in texture pattern.

Medium: 15 stitches in texture pattern, 2 Sweet, 2 Navy, 16 stitches in texture pattern, 2 Poison, 2 Sweet, 10 stitches in texture pattern.

Large: 15 stitches in texture pattern, 2 Sweet, 2 Navy, 16 stitches in texture pattern, 2 Poison, 2 Sweet, 16 stitches in texture pattern.

X-Large: 15 stitches texture pattern, 2 Sweet, 2 Navy, 16 stitches in texture pattern, 2 Poison, 2 Sweet, 16 stitches in texture pattern, 2 Sweet, 2 Navy, 3 stitches in texture pattern.

XX-Large: 15 stitches in texture pattern, 2 Sweet, 2 Navy, 16 stitches in texture pattern, 2 Poison, 2 Sweet, 16 stitches in texture pattern, 2 Sweet, 2 Navy, 9 stitches in texture pattern.

Working in pattern as set, cast on 3, 2, 2 stitches on the next and 2 following right-side rows (center front of Blazer), then 1 stitch on every following row (right side

and wrong side) 5 times, then on every right-side row twice, then on every other right-side row twice, taking increased stitches into stripe and texture pattern. 55(58, 65, 71, 78, 84) stitches. You should begin on the 11th stitch of the texture pattern and have another set of Poison and Sweet stripes, as on the Back. Decrease 1 stitch at the side edge (end of right-side rows) when the front measures 2 (2, 2, 2, 2½, 2½)" (5[5, 5, 5, 6.5, 6.5]cm), then repeat this decrease row three times more at 2" (5cm) intervals. 51(54, 61, 67, 74, 80) stitches. AT THE SAME TIME, when the front measures 2" (5cm) from the end of the center front shapings with the right side facing, make the first buttonhole:

Next row: Pattern 3, bind off 3, work in pattern to the end of the row.

Next row: In pattern, casting on 3 stitches over the 3 bound off. Make 4 more buttonholes in this way at the same time as working the rest of the shapings, spaced 3½" (9cm) apart.

Work even for 2½(2½, 2¾, 2¾, 2¾, 2¾)" (6.5[6.5, 7, 7, 7, 7]cm), ending with the wrong side facing for the next row.

Next row (increase): Increase 1 stitch at the side edge of the next row, work even for 2½" (6.5cm) (all sizes), work increase row again. 53(56, 63, 69, 76, 82) stitches. Work even until the back measures 15¾(16½, 17, 17¼, 17¼, 17¾)" (40[42, 43, 44, 44, 45]cm) from the cast-on edge, ending with the wrong side facing. Shape armholes, keeping pattern correct bind off:

X-Small: 3 stitches at the beginning of the next 2 wrong-side rows, then 2 on the next wrong-side rows. Decrease 1 stitch at the beginning of the next wrong-side row. AT THE SAME TIME, when front measures 18½" (47cm) from the cast-on edge with the right side facing, shape the front neck:

Decrease 1 stitch at the neck edge on the next and every following 3rd row until armhole measures 8" (20.5cm), when shoulder shaping begins. AT THE SAME TIME as continuing to decrease on every 3rd row at neck edge, bind off 3 stitches at beginning of next wrong-side row for shoulder, then 4 stitches at the beginning of next 5 wrong-side rows.

Small: 4 stitches at the beginning of the next wrong-side row, then 3 on the next wrong-side row, and 2 on the next wrong-side row. Decrease 1 stitch at the beginning of the next wrong-side row. AT THE SAME TIME, when front measures 18½" (47cm) from the cast-on edge with the right side facing, shape the front neck:

Decrease 1 stitch at the neck edge on the next and every following 3rd row until armhole measures 8¼" (21cm), when shoulder shaping begins. At the same time as continuing to decrease on every 3rd row at neck edge, bind off 4 stitches at the beginning of the next wrong-side row for shoulder, then 4 stitches at the beginning

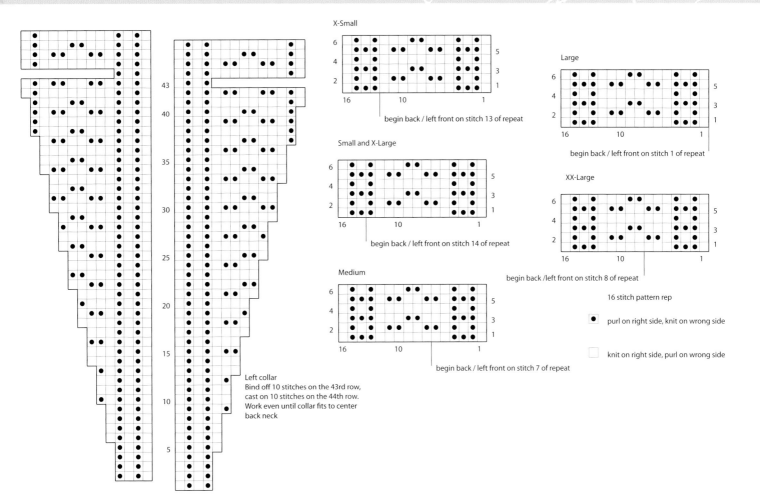

X-Small
begin back / left front on stitch 13 of repeat

Small and X-Large
begin back / left front on stitch 14 of repeat

Medium
begin back / left front on stitch 7 of repeat

Large
begin back / left front on stitch 1 of repeat

XX-Large
begin back /left front on stitch 8 of repeat

16 stitch pattern rep

● purl on right side, knit on wrong side

☐ knit on right side, purl on wrong side

Left collar
Bind off 10 stitches on the 43rd row,
cast on 10 stitches on the 44th row.
Work even until collar fits to center
back neck

of the next 3 wrong-side rows, work even at the neck edge from now on, bind off 4 stitches on the next wrong-side row and the remaining 5 stitches on the next wrong side.

Medium: 4 stitches at the beginning of the wrong-side row, then 3 on the next wrong-side row, then 2 on the next 2 wrong-side rows. Decrease 1 stitch at the beginning of the next 3 wrong-side rows. AT THE SAME TIME, when front measures 18½" (47cm) from the cast-on edge with the right side facing, shape the front neck:

Decrease 1 stitch at the neck edge on the next and every following 3rd row until armhole measures 8¼" (21cm), when shoulder shaping begins. AT THE SAME TIME as continuing to decrease on every 3rd row at neck edge, bind off 3 stitches at the beginning of the next wrong-side row for shoulder, then 4 stitches at the beginning of the next 5 wrong-side rows.

Large: 4 stitches at the beginning of the next 2 wrong-side rows, then 3 on the next

2 wrong-side rows, then 2 on the next 2 wrong-side rows. Decrease 1 stitch at the beginning of the next 3 wrong-side rows. AT THE SAME TIME, when front measures 18½" (47cm) from the cast-on edge with the right side facing, shape the front neck: Decrease 1 stitch at the neck edge on the next and every following 3rd row until armhole measures 8½" (22cm), when shoulder shaping begins. AT THE SAME TIME as continuing to decrease on every 3rd row at neck edge, bind off 4 stitches at the beginning of the next 4 wrong-side rows for shoulder, work even at the neck edge from now on, bind off 5 stitches at the beginning of the next 2 wrong-side rows.

X-Large: 5 stitches at the beginning of the next wrong-side row, then 4 on the next 2 wrong-side rows, then 3 on the next 3 wrong-side rows, and 2 on the next 2 wrong-side rows. Decrease 1 stitch at the beginning of the next wrong-side row. AT THE SAME TIME, when front measures 18½" (47cm) from the cast-on edge with the right side facing, shape the front neck:

Decrease 1 stitch at the neck edge on the next and every following 3rd row until armhole measures 8½" (22cm), when shoulder shaping begins. AT THE SAME TIME as continuing to decrease on every 3rd row at neck edge, bind off 4 stitches at the beginning of the next 4 wrong-side rows for shoulder, work even at the neck edge from now on, bind off 5 stitches at the beginning of the next 2 wrong-side rows.

XX-Large: 5 stitches on the next wrong-side row, then 4 on the next 3 wrong-side rows, 3 on the next 3 wrong-side rows, and 2 on the next 2 wrong-side rows. Decrease 1 stitch at the beginning of the next 2 wrong-side rows. AT THE SAME TIME, when front measures 18½" (47cm) from the cast-on edge with the right side facing, shape the front neck:

Decrease 1 stitch at the neck edge on the next and every following 3rd row until armhole measures 9" (23cm), when shoulder shaping begins. AT THE SAME TIME as continuing to decrease on every 3rd row at neck edge, bind off 4 stitches at the beginning of the next 3 wrong-side rows for shoulder, work even at the neck edge from now on, bind off 5 stitches at the beginning of the next 3 wrong-side rows.

Right sleeve

Cast on 56(56, 60, 64, 64, 66) stitches using Cream and size 6 (4mm) needles. Working from texture stitch chart appropriate for the size you are knitting, work:

X-Small: 14 texture, 2 Sweet, 2 Navy, 16 texture, 2 Poison, 2 Sweet, 14 texture. Increase at each end of the 5th and every following 6th row until there are 90 stitches, work even until sleeve measures 15" (38cm).

Small: 16 texture, 2 Sweet, 2 Navy, 16 texture, 2 Poison, 2 Sweet, 16 texture.

Medium: 18 texture, 2 Sweet, 2 Navy, 16 texture, 2 Poison, 2 Sweet, 18 texture.

Large and X-Large: 20 texture, 2 Sweet, 2 Navy, 16 texture, 2 Poison, 2 Sweet, 20 texture.

XX-Large: 1 texture, 2 Poison, 2 Sweet, 16 texture, 2 Sweet, 2 Navy, 16 texture, 2 Poison, 2 Sweet, 16 texture, 2 Sweet, 2 Navy, 1 texture.

Work in pattern as set, increase:

X-Small, Small, XX-Large: Increase at each end of the 5th and every following 6th row until there are 90 (92, 106) stitches. Work even until sleeve measures 15(15½, 17½)" (38 [39, 44.5]cm).

Medium: Increase at each end of the 9th row, then at each end of the following *6th row, then the following 8th row, repeat from * until there are 92 stitches, work even until sleeve measures 15½" (39cm).

Large, X-Large: Increase at each end of the 7th and every following 6th row until

there are 96(102) stitches, work even until sleeve measures 16(16½)" (40.5[42]cm).

Shape sleeve cap: Bind off 4(3, 3, 4, 4, 5) stitches at the beginning of the next 2 rows, then 3(3, 3, 3, 3, 4) stitches on the next 2 rows. Bind off 2(2, 2, 2, 2, 3) stitches at the beginning of the next 2 rows, then 2(2, 2, 2, 2, 2) stitches at the beginning of the following 2 rows.

X-Small, Small, Medium: Decrease 1 stitch at each end of every right-side row 14 times, now decrease on every other right-side row 4 times. Work 1(3, 3) rows even, bind off 2 stitches on the next 6(4, 4) rows, bind off the remaining 20 stitches on the next row for size X-Small, for Small and Medium bind off 3 stitches at the beginning of the next 2 rows, bind off the remaining 20 stitches.

Large, X-Large: Decrease 1 stitch at each end of the next 6 right-side rows, *work 3 rows even, decrease 1 stitch at each end of the next row 6 times. Decrease 1 stitch at each end of every right-side row 4(5) times more, work 3(0) rows even, bind off 2 stitches at the beginning of the next 6 rows, bind off 3(2) stitches at the beginning of the next 2 rows, bind off the remaining 20(22) stitches.

XX-Large: *Work 2 rows even, bind off 2 stitches at the beginning of the next 2 rows, repeat from * once more, work 2 rows even, decrease 1 stitch at each end of the next and every other right-side row 7 times, then every right-side row 6 times. Bind off 2 stitches at the beginning of the next 8 rows, bind off the remaining 24 stitches.

Left sleeve

Cast on 56(56, 60, 64, 64, 66) stitches using Cream and size 6 (4mm) needles. Working from texture stitch chart appropriate for the size you are knitting, work:

X-Small: 14 texture, 2 Poison, 2 Sweet, 16 texture, 2 Sweet, 2 Navy, 14 texture.

Small: 16 texture, 2 Poison, 2 Sweet, 16 texture, 2 Sweet, 2 Navy, 16 texture.

Medium: 18 texture, 2 Poison, 2 Sweet, 16 texture, 2 Sweet, 2 Navy, 18 texture.

Large and X-Large: 20 texture, 2 Poison, 2 Sweet, 16 texture, 2 Sweet, 2 Navy, 20 texture.

XX-Large: 1 texture, 2 Sweet, 2 Navy, 16 texture, 2 Poison, 2 Sweet, 16 texture, 2 Sweet, 2 Navy, 16 texture, 2 Poison, 2 Sweet, 1 texture.

Continue as for right sleeve.

Pocket

Cast on 35 stitches using Cream and size 6 (4mm) needles. Work in intarsia from chart for 42 rows, bind off.

Collar stand

Join shoulder seams. Mark a point 1" (2.5cm) down from the shoulder seam on each front. With the right side of the Blazer facing using size 5 (3.75mm) needles and Cream, pick up and knit 6 stitches from the point on the left front to the shoulder seam, 34(34, 36, 36, 36, 36) across back neck and 6 stitches down the right front to the point marked. Working 1 row in seed stitch.

Next 2 rows: Work in seed stitch to the last 4 stitches, wt.

Next 2 rows: Work in seed stitch to the last 8 stitches, wt.

Next 2 rows: Work in seed stitch to the last 12 stitches, wt.

Next row: Work in seed stitch to the end of the row, working wraps with the stitches they wrap.

Next row: Bind off in seed stitch, working the remaining wraps with the stitches they wrap as you bind them off.

Collar

Cast on 5 stitches using Cream and size 6 (4mm) needles. Work shaped collar sections as shown on chart, then work even until collar fits from center-front shaping to center-back of neck, bind off. Stitch neatly into place and join center back seam.

Cable trim

Cast on 3 stitches using Cream and 3 stitches using Navy and size 6 (4mm) needles. *Next row: k3 Navy, k3 Cream, twisting yarns together on the wrong side of work so that a hole is avoided.

Next row: P3 Cream, p3 Navy. Repeat these 2 rows once more.

Next row: Slip the 3 Navy stitches to a cable needle and hold at the back of the work, k3 in Cream, k3 in Navy from the cable needle.

Next row: P3 Navy, p3 Cream.

Next row: K3 Cream, k3 Navy. Repeat these 2 rows once more.

Next row: Slip the 3 Cream stitches to a cable needle and hold at the back of the work, k3 Navy, k3 Cream.

Next row: P3 Cream, p3 Navy. Repeat from * until braid is long enough to reach across back hem, around right front, collar, and left front. Bind off and slip stitch neatly into place. Make 2 more braids to go around cuffs, and one to fit across pocket top. Slip stitch into place. Sew in sleeves, sew side and sleeve seams, sew pocket neatly onto left front as in the photograph.

Finishing

Sew on buttons, sew in all ends.

Cricket Blazer Pocket chart

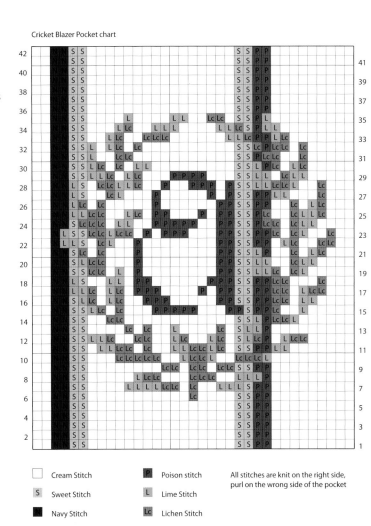

☐ Cream Stitch

S Sweet Stitch

■ Navy Stitch

P Poison stitch

L Lime Stitch

Lc Lichen Stitch

All stitches are knit on the right side, purl on the wrong side of the pocket

Skill level: Easy.

Size S(M, L, XL).

Finished Chest: 40(44, 48, 52)" (101.5[112, 117, 132])cm.

Materials:

29(30, 30, 31) balls of RYC Cashsoft Aran, 57% Extra Fine Merino Wool, 33% Microfiber, 10% Cashmere 🔲 medium [1¾ oz (50g), 95yd (87m)], 23(24, 24, 25), Cream, 2 each of Thunder, Mist, and Navy. Size 7(4.5mm) and 5 (3.75mm) straight needles, size 5 (3.75mm) 16" (41cm) circular needle, cable needle.

Gauge: 29 stitches and 26 rows to 4" (10cm) over cable pattern on size 7 (4.5mm) needles.

End over end cable—a panel of 10 stitches.

Front cross—Fc6.

Rows 1, 3, and 7: P2, k6, p2.

Rows 2, 4, 6, and 8: K2, p6, k2.

Row 5: P2, slip the next 6 stitches to a cable needle and twist ½ turn clockwise, k6 from cable needle, p2.

Repeat rows 1–8.

Back cross—bc6.

Rows 1, 3, and 7: P2, k6, p2.

Rows 2, 4, 6, and 8: K2, p6, k2.

Row 5: P2, slip the next 6 stitches to a cable needle and twist ½ turn counter-clockwise, k6 from cable needle, p2.

Repeat rows 1–8.

"Rope" cable—a panel of 4 stitches.

Front cross—C4f.

Row 1: Knit.

Rows 2 and 4: Purl.

Row 3: Slip the first 2 stitches to a cable needle and hold at the front of the work, k2, k2 from the cable needle.

Back cross—C4b.

Row 1: Knit.

Rows 2 and 4: Purl.

Row 3: Slip the first 2 stitches to a cable needle and hold at the back of the work, k2, k2 from the cable needle.

Tiny twisted cables "t2f/b"—worked over 2 stitches.

Place the stitches onto a cable needle on every right-side row of the work, twist then a ½ turn clockwise for t2f, and twist them counterclockwise for a t2b. Purl on the wrong side of the work.

Front

Cast on 120(128, 136, 144) stitches using Cream and size 5 (3.75mm) needles.

Small:

Row 1: P1, k4, p2, k4, p2, k4, p2, k4, p2, [p2, k4, p2, k4, p2], p2, k4, p2, k4, p2, rep [ ], p2, k4, p2, k4, p2, rep [ ], p2, k4, p2, k4, p2, k4, p2, k4, p1.

Rows 2 and 4: Work stitches as they face you.

Row 3: P1, c4b, p2, c4b, p2, c4b, p2, c4b, p2, [p2, c4b, p2, c4b, p2], p2, c4b, p2, c4b, p2, (p2, c4b, p2, c4f, p2), p2, c4f, p2, c4f, p2, repeat [ ] but working c4f on both cables, p2, c4f, p2, c4f, p2, c4f, p1.

Medium:

Row 1: K1, p4, k4, p2, k4, p2, k4, p2, k4, p2, [p2, k4, p2, k4, p2], p2, k4, p2, k4, p2, repeat [ ], p2, k4, p2, k4, p2, repeat [ ], p2, k4, p2, k4, p2, k4, p2, k4, p4, k1.

Rows 2 and 4: Work stitches as they face you.

Row 3: K1, p4, c4b, p2, c4b, p2, c4b, p2, c4b, p2, [p2, c4b, p2, c4b, p2], p2, c4b, p2, c4b, p2, (p2, c4b, p2, c4f, p2), p2, c4f, p2, c4f, p2, repeat [ ] but working c4f on both cables, p2, c4f, p2, c4f, p2, c4f, p4, k1.

Large:

Row 1: P3, k4, p2, k4, p2, k4, p2, k4, p2, k4, p2, [p2, k4, p2, k4, p2], p2, k4, p2, k4, p2, repeat [ ], p2, k4, p2, k4, p2, repeat [ ], p2, k4, p2, k4, p2, k4, p2, k4, p2, k4, p3.

Rows 2 and 4: Work stitches as they face you.

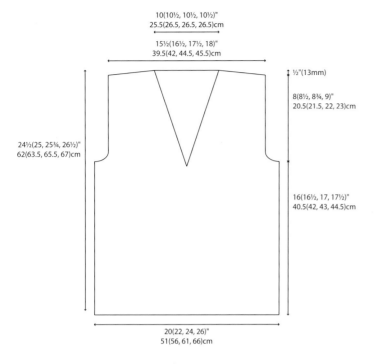

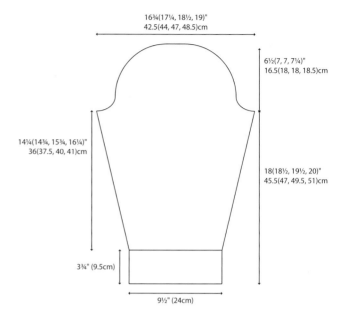

Row 3: P3, c4b, p2, c4b, p2, c4b, p2, c4b, p2, c4b, p2, [p2, c4b, p2, c4b, p2], p2, c4b, p2, c4b, p2, (p2, c4b, p2, c4f, p2), p2, c4f, p2, c4f, p2, repeat [ ] but working c4f on both cables, p2, c4f, p2, c4f, p2, c4f, p2, c4f, p3.

X-Large:

Row 1: P1, k4, p2, k4, p2, k4, p2, k4, p2, k4, p2, k4, p2, [p2, k4, p2, k4, p2], p2, k4, p2, k4, p2, repeat [ ], p2, k4, p2, k4, p2, repeat [ ], p2, k4, p2, k4, p2, k4, p2, k4, p2, k4, p2, k4, p1.

Rows 2 and 4: Work stitches as they face you.

Row 3: P1, c4b, p2, c4b, p2, c4b, p2, c4b, p2, c4b, p2, c4b, p2, [p2, c4b, p2, c4b, p2], p2, c4b, p2, c4b, p2, (p2, c4b, p2, c4f, p2), p2, c4f, p2, c4f, p2, repeat [ ] but working c4f on both cables, p2, c4f, p2, c4f, p2, c4f, p2, c4f, p1.

These 4 rows repeat for the cable ribbing, work 8 rows Cream, 4 rows Mist, 4 rows Navy, 8 rows Thunder, 4 rows Navy, 3 rows Mist, end with the wrong side facing for the next (increase) row:

Small: K1, p4, k2, pfb, p3, k2, pfb, p3, k2, pfb, p3, k4, [p1, m1p, p2, m1p, p1] k2 repeat [ ], k4, pfb, p2, pfb, k2, pfb, p2, pfb, k4, repeat [ ], k2 repeat [ ], k4, pfb, p2, pfb, k2, pfb, p2, pfb, k4 repeat [ ], k2 repeat [ ], k4, p3, pfb, k2, p3, pfb, k2, p3, pfb, k2 p4, k1. 146 stitches.

Medium: P1, k4, p3, pfb, k2, p3, pfb, k2, pfb, p2, pfb, , k2, pfb,p2, pfb, k4 [p1, m1p, p2, m1p, p1] k2, repeat [ ], k4, pfb, p2, pfb, k2, pfb, p2, pfb, k4, repeat [ ], k2, repeat [ ], k4, pfb, p2, pfb, k2, pfb, p2, pfb, k4, repeat [ ], k2, repeat [ ], k4, pfb, p2, pfb, k2, pfb, p2, pfb, k2, pfb, p3, k2, pfb, p3, k4, p1. 160 stitches.

Large: K3, p3, pfb, k2, pfb, p2, pfb, k2, pfb, p2, pfb, k2, pfb, p2, pfb, k2, pfb, p2, pfb, k4, [p1, m1p, p2, m1p, p1] k2, repeat [ ], k4, pfb, p2, pfb, k2, pfb, p2, pfb, k4, repeat [ ], k2, repeat [ ], k4, pfb, p2, pfb, k2, pfb, p2, pfb, k4, repeat [ ], k2, repeat [ ], k4, pfb, p2, pfb, k2, pfb, p2, pfb, k2, pfb, p2, pfb, k2, pfb, p3, k3. 174 stitches.

X-Large: K1, pfb, p2, pfb (k2, pfb, p2, pfb) 5 times, k4, [p1, m1p, p2, m1p, p1] k2, repeat [ ], k4, pfb, p2, pfb, k2, pfb, p2, pfb, k4, repeat [ ], k2, repeat [ ] k4, pfb, p2, pfb, k2, pfb, p2, pfb, k4, repeat [ ], k2, repeat [ ], k4, (pfb, p2, pfb, k2) 5 times, end pfb, p2, pfb, k1. 188 stitches.

Change to size 7 (4.5mm) needles and Cream yarn and begin body cable pattern:

Small:

Row 1: K1, t2b, p2, t2b, p2. k4, p2, t2b, p2, t2b, p2, k4, p2, k6, p2, k6, p2, k4, p2, t2b, p2, t2b, p2, k4, p2, k6, p2, k6, p2, k4, p2, t2f, p2, t2f, p2, k4, p2, k6, p2, k6, p2, k4, p2, t2f, p2, t2f, p2, k4, p2, t2f, p2, t2f, k1.

Row 2 (and all wrong-side rows): Work stitches as they face you.

Row 3: K1, t2b, p2, t2b, p2, c4b, p2, t2b, p2, t2b, p2, c4f, p2, k6, p2, k6, p2, c4b, p2, t2b, p2, t2b, p2, c4f, p2, k6, p2, k6, p2, c4b, p2, t2f, p2, t2f, p2, c4f, p2, k6, p2, k6, p2, c4b, p2, t2f, p2, t2f, p2, c4f, p2, t2f, p2, t2f, k1.

Row 5: K1, t2b, p2, t2b, p2, k4, p2, t2b, p2, t2b, p2, k4, p2, fc6, p2, bc6, p2, k4, p2, t2b, p2, t2b, p2, k4, p2, fc6, p2, bc6, p2, k4, p2, t2f, p2, t2f, p2, k4, p2, fc6, p2, bc6, p2, k4, p2, t2f, p2, t2f, p2, k4, p2, t2f, p2, t2f, k1.

Medium:

Row 1: K1, p2, k4, p2, t2b, p2, t2b, p2, k4, p2, t2b, p2, t2b, p2, k4, p2, k6, p2, k6, p2, k4, p2, t2b, p2, t2b, p2, k4, p2, k6, p2, k6, p2, k4, p2, t2f, p2, t2f, p2, k4, p2, k6, p2, k6, p2, k4, p2, t2f, p2, t2f, p2, k4, p2, t2f, p2, t2f, p2, k4, p2, k1.

Row 2 (and all wrong-side rows): Work stitches as they face you.

Row 3: K1, p2, c4f, p2, t2b, p2, t2b, p2, c4b, p2, t2b, p2, t2b, p2, c4f, p2, k6, p2, k6, p2, c4b, p2, t2b, p2, t2b, p2, c4f, p2, k6, p2, k6, p2, c4b, p2, t2f, p2, t2f, p2, c4f, p2, k6, p2, k6, p2, c4b, p2, t2f, p2, t2f, p2, c4f, p2, t2f, p2, t2f, p2, c4f, p2, k1.

Row 5: K1, p2, k4, p2, t2b, p2, t2b, p2, k4, p2, t2b, p2, t2b, p2, k4, p2, fc6, p2, bc6, p2, k4, p2, t2b, p2, t2b, p2, k4, p2, fc6, p2, bc6, p2, k4, p2, t2f, p2, t2f, p2, k4, p2, fc6, p2, bc6, p2, k4, p2, t2f, p2, t2f, p2, k4, p2, t2f, p2, t2f, p2, k4, p2, k1.

Large:

Row 1: P2, t2b, p2, t2b, p2, k4, p2, t2b, p2, t2b, p2, k4, p2, t2b, p2, t2b, p2, k4, p2, k6, p2, k6, p2, k4, p2, t2b, p2, t2b, p2, k4, p2, k6, p2, k6, p2, k4, p2, t2f, p2, t2f, p2, k4, p2, k6, p2, k6, p2, k4, p2, t2f, p2, t2f, p2, k4, p2, t2f, p2, t2f, p2.

Row 2 (and all wrong-side rows): Work stitches as they face you.

Row 3: P2, t2b, p2, t2b, p2, c4f, p2, t2b, p2, t2b, p2, c4f, p2, t2b, p2, t2b, p2, c4f, p2, k6, p2, k6, p2, c4f, p2, t2b, p2, t2b, p2, k4, p2, k6, p2, k6, p2, c4b, p2, t2f, p2, t2f, p2, c4b, p2, k6, p2, k6, p2, c4b, p2, t2f, p2, t2f, p2, c4b, p2, t2f, p2, t2f, p2.

Row 5: P2, t2b, p2, t2b, p2, k4, p2, t2b, p2, t2b, p2, k4, p2, t2b, p2, t2b, p2, k4, p2, fc6, p2, bc6, p2, k4, p2, t2b, p2, t2b, p2, k4, p2, fc6, p2, bc6, p2, k4, p2, t2f, p2, t2f, p2, k4, p2, fc6, p2, bc6, p2, k4, p2, t2f, p2, t2f, p2, k4, p2, t2f, p2, t2f, p2.

X-Large:

Row 1: K1, p2, k4, p2, t2b, p2, t2b, p2, k4, p2, t2b, p2, t2b, p2, k4, p2, t2b, p2, t2b, p2, k4, p2, k6, p2, k6, p2, k4, p2, t2b, p2, t2b, p2, k4, p2, k6, p2, k6, p2, k4, p2, t2f,

p2, t2f, p2, k4, p2, k6, p2, k6, p2, k4, p2, t2f, p2, t2f, p2, k4, p2, t2f, p2, t2f, p2, k4, p2, t2f, p2, t2f, p2, k4, p2, k1.

Row 2 (and all wrong-side rows): Work stitches as they face you.

Row 3: K1, p2, c4f, p2, t2b, p2, t2b, p2, c4f, p2, t2b, p2, t2b, p2, c4f, p2, t2b, p2, t2b, p2, c4f, p2, k6, p2, k6, p2, c4f, p2, t2b, p2, t2b, p2, k4, p2, k6, p2, k6, p2, c4b, p2, t2f, p2, t2f, p2, c4b, p2, k6, p2, k6, p2, c4b, p2, t2f, p2, t2f, p2, c4b, p2, t2f, p2, t2f, p2, c4f, p2, k1.

Row 5: K1, p2, k4, p2, t2b, p2, t2b, p2, k4, p2, t2b, p2, t2b, p2, k4, p2, t2b, p2, t2b, p2, k4, p2, fc6, p2, bc6, p2, k4, p2, t2b, p2, t2b, p2, k4, p2, fc6, p2, bc6, p2, k4, p2, t2f, p2, t2f, p2, k4, p2, fc6, p2, bc6, p2, k4, p2, t2f, p2, t2f, p2, k4, p2, t2f, p2, t2f, p2, k4, p2, t2f, p2, t2f, p2, k4, p2, k1.

Cable repeats now set. Continue until front measures 14½(15¼, 16, 16½)" (37[38.5, 40.5, 42]cm) from cast-on edge*. Split for neck shaping:

Next row: Pattern 73(80, 87, 94), turn. Work 1 row (right side of work is now facing for the next row).

Next row (right side): Work in pattern to the last 11 stitches, k2tog, pattern 9.

Next row: Work even.

Next row: Decrease as before.

Next row: Work even.

Next row: Work even.

Next row (wrong side): Pattern 9, ssk (or ssp), work in pattern to the end of the row.

These 6 rows repeat for the neck decreases and AT THE SAME TIME, when the front measures 16(16½ 17, 17½)" (40.5[42, 43, 44.5]cm), begin armhole decreases:

Small: Bind off 3, 2, 2, 1 stitches at the beginning of the next 4 right-side rows.

Medium: Bind off 4, 3, 2, 2 stitches at the beginning of the next 4 right-side rows.

Large: Bind off 4, 3, 3, 2, 1, 1, 1, 1 stitches at the beginning of the next 8 right-side rows.

X-Large: Bind off 4, 4, 3, 3, 2, 1, 1, 1, 1, 1 stitches at the beginning of the next 10 right-side rows.

Work neck decreases until 28(31, 33, 35) stitches remain for the shoulder. Work even until the armhole measures 8(8½, 8¾, 9)" (20.5[21.5, 22, 23]cm), work shoulder shaping:

Small: Bind off 10, 9, 9 stitches at the beginning of the next 3 right-side rows.

Medium: Bind off 11, 10, 10 stitches at the beginning of the next 3 right-side rows.

Large: Bind off 11 stitches at the beginning of the next 3 right-side rows.

X-Large: Bind off 12, 12, 11 stitches at the beginning of the next 3 right-side rows.

Rejoin yarn to the remaining stitches and work the right side of the neck:

Next row: Work in pattern to the end. Work 1 row (right side of work is now facing for the next row).

Next row (right side): Pattern 9, ssk, work in pattern to the end.

Next row: Work even.

Next row: Decrease as before.

Next row: Work even.

Next row: Work even.

Next row (wrong side): Work in pattern to the last 11 stitches, p2tog (or k2tog), pattern 9.

These 6 rows repeat for the neck decreases and AT THE SAME TIME, when the front measures 16(16½ 17, 17½)" (40.5[42, 43, 44.5]cm), begin armhole decreases:

Small: Bind off 3, 2, 2, 1 stitches at the beginning of the next 4 wrong-side rows.

Medium: Bind off 4, 3, 2, 2 stitches at the beginning of the next 4 wrong-side rows.

Large: Bind off 4, 3, 3, 2, 1, 1, 1, 1 stitches at the beginning of the next 8 wrong-side rows.

X-Large: Bind off 4, 4, 3, 3, 2, 1, 1, 1, 1, 1 stitches at the beginning of the next 10 wrong-side rows.

Work neck decreases until 28(31, 33, 35) stitches remain for the shoulder. Work even until the armhole measures 8(8½, 8¾, 9)" (20.5[21.5, 22, 23]cm), work shoulder shaping:

Small: Bind off 10, 9, 9 stitches at the beginning of the next 3 wrong-side rows.

Medium: Bind off 11, 10, 10 stitches at the beginning of the next 3 wrong-side rows.

Large: Bind off 11 stitches at the beginning of the next 3 wrong-side rows.

X-Large: Bind off 12, 12, 11 stitches at the beginning of the next 3 wrong-side rows.

Back

Work as for front until *. Work even until back measures 16(16½ 17, 17½)" (40.5[42, 43, 44.5]cm), begin armhole decreases:

Small: Bind off 3 stitches at the beginning of the next 2 rows, 2 stitches on the next 4 rows, and decrease 1 stitch at each end of the next row. 128 stitches.

Medium: Bind off 4 stitches at the beginning of the next 2 rows, then 3 stitches at the beginning of the following 2 rows, 2 stitches at the beginning of the following 4 rows. 138 stitches.

Large: Bind off 4 stitches at the beginning of the next 2 rows, 3 stitches on the next 4 rows, 2 stitches on the next 2 rows, and decrease 1 stitch at each end of the next 4 rows. 142 stitches.

X-Large: Bind off 4 stitches at the beginning of the next 4 rows, 3 stitches on the following 4 rows, 2 stitches on the next 2 rows, and decrease 1 stitch at each end of the next 5 right-side rows. 146 stitches.

Work even until the back matches the front to the beginning of the shoulder shaping, shape shoulders.

Small: Bind off 10 stitches at the beginning of the next 2 rows and 9 stitches on the next 4 rows. 72 stitches.

Medium: Bind off 11 stitches at the beginning of the next 2 rows and 10 stitches on the next 4 rows. 76 stitches.

Large: Bind off 11 stitches at the beginning of the next 6 rows. 76 stitches.

X-Large: Bind off 12 stitches at the beginning of the next 4 rows, then 11 stitches on the next 2 rows. 76 stitches.

Leave the remaining stitches on a holder for the back neck.

Sleeves

Cast on 70 stitches for all sizes using size 5 (3.75mm) needles and Cream.

Row 1: P2, k4, p2, k4, p2, p2, k4, p2, k4, p2, p2, k4, p2, k4, p2, p2, k4, p2, k4, p2, p2, k4, p2, k4, p2.

Row 2: As set.

Row 3: P2, c4f, p2, c4f, p2, p2, c4f, p2, c4f, p2, p2, c4f, p2, c4b, p2, p2, c4b, p2, c4b, p2, p2, c4b, p2, c4b, p2.

Repeat cable pattern as for back and front, but work stripes:

6 rows Cream, 4 Mist, 4 Navy, 6 Thunder, 4 Navy, 3 Mist, ending with the wrong side facing for the next (increase) row:

Next (increase) row: K2, p1, m1, p2, m1, p2, m1, k2, p1, m1, p2, m1, p1, kfb, kfb, p4, k2, p4, kfb, kfb, k2, p1, m1, p2, m1, p1, k2, p1, m1, p2, m1, p1, k2, kfb,

kfb, p4, k2, p4, kfb, kfb, k2, p1, m1, p2, m1, p1, k2, p1, m1, p2, m1, p2. 90 stitches.

Change to size 7 (4.5mm) needles and Cream, and work in cable pattern:

Row 1: P2, k6, p2, k6, p2, k4, p2, t2b, p2, t2b, p2, k4, p2, k6, p2, k6, p2, k4, p2, t2f, p2, t2f, p2, k4, p2, k6, p2, k6, p2.

Work cables as set, increasing 1 stitch at each end of the 5th row, then on every following 4th row, until there are 122(126, 134, 138) stitches, taking the increased stitches into the t2f/b, p2 pattern on either side.

Work even until the sleeve measures 18(18½, 19½, 20)" (45.5[47, 49.5, 51]cm) from the cast-on edge, ending with the right side facing. Shape sleeve cap:

Small and Medium: Bind off 4, 3, 2, 2, stitches at the beginning of the next 8 rows. Decrease 1 stitch at each end of every row until 30 stitches remain, bind off.

Large and X-Large: Bind off 4, 4, 3, 2, 2, stitches at the beginning of the next 10 rows. Decrease 1 stitch at each end of every row until 32 stitches remain, bind off.

Neckband

Sew shoulder seams. With size 5 (3.75mm) circular needle and Cream, pick up and knit 45(45, 45, 45) stitches down left side of front neck, 45(45, 45, 45) stitches up right side of neck, 72(76, 76, 76) stitches across back neck. 132(136, 136, 136) stitches.

Working in k2, p2 ribbing in rounds, work stripes and decreases as follows:

Round 1 in Cream: *K2, p2, repeat from * until 44(44, 44, 44) stitches have been worked, place marker, k2, place marker, rib to end.

Round 2 in Mist: Rib to 2 stitches before the1st marker, work 2 stitches together, slip marker, k2, slip marker, work 2 stitches together, rib to end.

Round 3 in Navy: Work even.

Round 4 in Thunder: Work decrease round.

Round 5 in Thunder: Work even.

Round 6 in Navy: Work decrease round.

Round 7 in Mist: Work even.

Round 8 in Cream: Work decrease round.

Round 9 in Cream: Bind off in rib.

Finishing

Set in sleeves, sew side and sleeve seams. Weave in all ends.

Skill level: Intermediate.

Size: S(M, L, XL, XXL).

Finished Bust: 34(38, 42, 46, 50)" (86[96.5, 106.5, 117, 127]cm).

Materials:

15(16, 17, 17, 18) balls RYC Silk Wool DK, 50% Silk, 50% Merino Wool, [1¾ oz (50g), 109yd (100m)], Milk. **(3)** light
Size 5 (3.75mm) and 7 (4.5mm) needles. Cable needle.

Gauge: 34 stitches and 28 rows to 4" (10cm) over cable panels A and B with 1 twisted stitch
and 1 reverse stockinette stitch between them on size 7(4.5mm) needles.

NOTE: Although the stitch counts on the back and front are different because the cables on the back do not "draw in"
as much as the ones on the front do, the two pieces come out the same size.

Front

Cast on 130(146, 160, 170, 190) stitches using size 5 (3.75mm) needles. Work 19 rows in k2, p2 rib**. Increase on the next (wrong side) row:

Small and X-Large: (Rib 10, m1p) 12(16) times, rib 10. 142(186) stitches.

Medium: *Rib12, m1, (rib11, m1p) 5 times, repeat from * once, end rib 12. 158 stitches.

Large: Rib 14, m1, (rib12, m1p) 11 times, end rib 14. 172 stitches.

XX-Large: (Rib 9, m1p) 20 times, end rib 10. 210 stitches.

Change to size 7(4.5mm) needles and work in cable pattern as follows for Small,

Medium, Large, X-Large:

Row 1: (K1, p1) 6(10, 14, 17) times, k1(1, 0, 1), k1tbl, work row 1 of chart A, k1tbl, p2, work row 1 of chart B, p2, k1tbl, work row 1 of chart C, k1tbl, p2, work row 1 chart B, p2, k1tbl, work row 1 of chart A, k1tbl, (k1, p1) 6 (10, 14, 17) times, k1 (1, 0, 1).

Row 2: (K1, p1) 6(10, 14, 17) times, k1(1, 0, 1), p1tbl, work row 2 chart A, p1tbl, k2, work row 2 chart B, k2, p1tbl, work row 2 of chart C, p1tbl, k2, work row 2 of chart B, k2, p1tbl, work row 2 of chart A, p1tbl, (k1, p1) 6(10, 14, 17) times, k1(1, 0, 1).

13(21, 28, 35) stitches of seed stitch repeat at each side of work.

XX-Large:

Row 1: (K1, p1) 7 times, k1, k1tbl, work row 1 of chart B, p2, k1tbl, p2, work row 1 of chart B, p2, k1tbl, work row 1 of chart A, k1tbl, p2, work row 1 of chart B, p2, k1tbl, work row 1 of chart C, k1tbl, p2, work row 1 of chart B, p2, k1tbl, work row 1 of chart A, k1tbl, p2, work row 1 of chart B, p2, k1tbl, p2, work row 1 of chart B, p2, k1tbl, (k1, p1) 7 times, k1.

Row 2: (K1, p1) 7 times, k1, p1tbl, work row 2 of chart B, k2, p1tbl, k2, work row 2 of chart B, k2, p1tbl, work row 2 of chart A, p1tbl, k2, work row 2 of chart B, k2, p1tbl, work row 2 of chart C, p1tbl, k2, work row 1 of chart B, k2, p1tbl, work row 2 of chart A, p1tbl, k2, work row 2 of chart B, k2, p1tbl, k2, work row 2 of chart B, k2, p1tbl, (k1, p1) 7 times, k1.

15 stitches of seed stitch repeat at each side of the work.

Work in pattern as set, decrease 1 stitch (pattern 2 together, work in pattern to last 2 stitches, pattern 2 together) at each end of the next and every following 4th row until there are 118(130, 148, 158, 182) stitches. Work even until the front measures 10(10, 11, 11½, 11½)" (25.5[25.5, 28, 29, 29]cm). Increase 1 stitch (kfb, k to last stitch, kfb) at each end of next and every following 4th row until there are 136(144, 162, 172, 196) stitches, work even until the front measures 15(15½, 15½, 16, 16½)" ([38[39.5, 39.5, 40.5, 42]cm) from the cast-on edge with the right side facing for the next row.

Small and Medium: Bind off 3 stitches at the beginning of the next 2 rows, then 2 stitches at the beginning of the next 4 rows, and 1 stitch at the beginning of the next 2 rows. 120(128) stitches.

Large: Bind off 4 stitches at the beginning of the next 2 rows, 3 stitches at the beginning of the next 2 rows, 2 stitches on the next 4 rows, and 1 stitch on the next 2 rows. 138 stitches.

X-Large: Bind off 5 stitches at the beginning of the next 2 rows, 4 stitches on the next 2 rows, then 3 stitches on the next 2 rows, and 2 stitches on the next 2 rows. Bind off 1 stitch at the beginning of the next 6 rows. 138 stitches.

XX-Large: Bind off 5 stitches at the beginning of the next 2 rows, 4 stitches on the

SOMERSET CABLE SWEATER

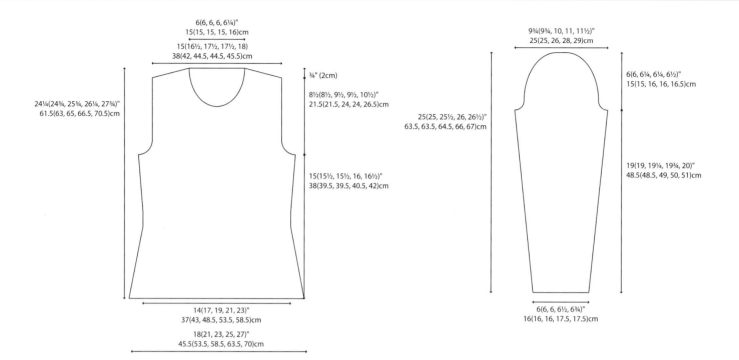

6(6, 6, 6, 6¼)"
15(15, 15, 15, 16)cm

15(16½, 17½, 17½, 18)
38(42, 44.5, 44.5, 45.5)cm

24¼(24¾, 25¾, 26¼, 27¾)"
61.5(63, 65, 66.5, 70.5)cm

¾" (2cm)

8½(8½, 9½, 9½, 10½)"
21.5(21.5, 24, 24, 26.5)cm

15(15½, 15½, 16, 16½)"
38(39.5, 39.5, 40.5, 42)cm

14(17, 19, 21, 23)"
37(43, 48.5, 53.5, 58.5)cm

18(21, 23, 25, 27)"
45.5(53.5, 58.5, 63.5, 70)cm

9¾(9¾, 10, 11, 11½)"
25(25, 26, 28, 29)cm

6(6, 6¼, 6¼, 6½)"
15(15, 16, 16, 16.5)cm

25(25, 25½, 26, 26½)"
63.5(63.5, 64.5, 66, 67)cm

19(19, 19¼, 19¾, 20)"
48.5(48.5, 49, 50, 51)cm

6(6, 6, 6½, 6¾)"
16(16, 16, 17.5, 17.5)cm

next 2 rows, 3 stitches at the beginning of the next 4 rows, 2 stitches on the following 4 rows, and 1 stitch at the beginning of the next 16 rows. 142 stitches. Work even until the armhole measures 4½(4½, 5, 5, 5½)" (11.5[11.5, 12.5, 12.5, 14]cm) with the right side facing for the next row.

Shape front neck

Pattern 50(54, 59, 59, 61), bind off the next 20 stitches, work in pattern to the end of the row. Work 1 row even. Bind off 3, 3, 2, 2, 2, 2, 1, 1, 1 stitches at the beginning of the next 9 right-side rows, then 0(0, 0, 0, 1) stitch twice on the next 2 rows. 33(37, 42, 42, 42) stitches. Work 1 row even, wrong side is now facing for the beginning of the shoulder shaping. Keeping the neck edge straight from now on, bind off 11(12, 14, 14, 14) stitches at the beginning of the next row, work 1 row even, 11(12, 14, 14, 14) stitches at the beginning of the next row, work 1 row even, bind off the remaining 11(13, 14, 14, 14) stitches.

With the wrong side of the work facing, rejoin yarn to the remaining stitches and work the right side of the neck:

Work 1 row even. Bind off 3, 3, 2, 2, 2, 2, 1, 1, 1 stitches at the beginning of the next 9 wrong-side rows, then 0(0, 0, 0, 1) stitch twice on the next 2 rows. 33(37, 42, 42, 42) stitches. Work 1 row even, right side is now facing for the beginning of the

shoulder shaping. Keeping the neck edge straight from now on, bind off 11(12, 14, 14, 14) stitches at the beginning of the next row, work 1 row even, 11(12, 14, 14, 14) stitches at the beginning of the next row, work 1 row even, bind off the remaining 11(13, 14, 14, 14) stitches.

Back

Work as for front until **. Increase on the next (wrong side) row:

Small: Rib 15, m1p, (rib 11, m1p) 4 times, rib 12, m1p, (rib 11 m1p) 4 times, rib to end. 140 stitches.

Medium: *Rib 14, m1p, (rib 13, m1p) 4 times, repeat from *, end rib 14. 156 stitches.

Large: (Rib 15, m1p, rib 14, m1p) 5 times, end rib 15. 170 stitches.

X-Large: (Rib 12, m1p, rib11, m1p) 3 times, (rib 11, m1p) 4 times, (rib 12, m1p, rib 11, m1p) twice, end rib 12. 184 stitches.

XX-Large: *Rib 12, m1p, (rib 11, m1p) 7 times, repeat from *, end rib 12. 206 stitches.

Change to 4.5mm needles and work in cable pattern as follows:

Change to size 7 (4.5mm) needles and work in cable pattern as follows for **Small, Medium, Large, X-Large:**

Row 1: (K1, p1) 6(10, 14, 17) times, k1(1, 0, 1), k1tbl, work row 1 of chart A, k1tbl,

58   **KNITTING AND TEA**

p2, work row 1 of chart B, p2, k1tbl, work row 1 of chart A twice, k1tbl, p2, work row 1 chart B, p2, k1tbl, work row 1 of chart A, k1tbl, (k1, p1) 6 (10, 14, 17) times, k1 (1, 0, 1).

Row 2: (K1, p1) 6(10, 14, 17) times, k1(1, 0, 1), p1tbl, work row 2 chart A, p1tbl, k2, work row 2 chart B, k2, p1tbl, work row 2 of chart A twice, p1tbl, k2, work row 2 of chart B, k2, p1tbl, work row 2 of chart A, p1tbl, (k1, p1) 6(10, 14, 17) times, k1(1, 0, 1).

13(21, 28, 35) stitches of seed stitch repeat at each side of work.

XX-Large:

Row 1: (K1, p1) 7 times, k1, k1tbl, work row 1 of chart B, p2, k1tbl, p2, work row 1 of chart B, p2, k1tbl, work row 1 of chart A, k1tbl, p2, work row 1 of chart B, p2, k1tbl, work row 1 of chart A twice, k1tbl, p2, work row 1 of chart B, p2, k1tbl, work row 1 of chart A, k1tbl, p2, work row 1 of chart B, p2, k1tbl, p2, work row 1 of chart B, p2, k1tbl, (k1, p1) 7 times, k1.

Row 2: (K1, p1) 7 times, k1, p1tbl, work row 2 of chart B, k2, p1tbl, k2, work row 2 of chart B, k2, p1tbl, work row 2 of chart A, p1tbl, k2, work row 2 of chart B, k2, p1tbl, work row 2 of chart A twice, p1tbl, k2, work row 1 of chart B, k2, p1tbl, work row 2 of chart A, p1tbl, k2, work row 2 of chart B, k2, p1tbl, k2, work row 2 of chart B, k2, p1tbl, (k1, p1) 7 times, k1.

15 stitches of seed stitch repeat at each side of the work.

Work in pattern as set, decrease 1 stitch (pattern 2 together, work in pattern to last 2 stitches, pattern 2 together) at each end of the next and every following 4th row until there are 116(128, 142, 156, 178) stitches. Work even until the back measures 10(10, 11, 11½, 11½)" (25.5[25.5, 28, 29, 29]cm). Increase 1 stitch (kfb, k to last stitch, kfb) at each end of next and every following 4th row until there are 134(142, 156, 170, 192) stitches, work even until the back measures 15(15½, 15½, 16, 16½)" ([38(39.5, 39.5, 40.5, 42]cm) from the cast-on edge with the right side facing for the next row.

Small and Medium: Bind off 3 stitches at the beginning of the next 2 rows, then 2 stitches at the beginning of the next 4 rows, and 1 stitch at the beginning of the next 2 rows. 118(126) stitches.

Large: Bind off 4 stitches at the beginning of the next 2 rows, 3 stitches at the beginning of the next 2 rows, 2 stitches on the next 4 rows, and 1 stitch on the next 2 rows. 134 stitches.

X-Large: Bind off 5 stitches at the beginning of the next 2 rows, 4 stitches

on the next 2 rows, then 3 stitches on the next 2 rows, and 2 stitches on the next 2 rows. Bind off 1 stitch at the beginning of the next 6 rows. 136 stitches.

XX-Large: Bind off 5 stitches at the beginning of the next 2 rows, 4 stitches on the next 2 rows, 3 stitches at the beginning of the next 4 rows, 2 stitches on the following 4 rows, and 1 stitch at the beginning of the next 16 rows. 138 stitches. Work even until armholes match front armholes to beginning of shoulder shaping, with the right side facing. Bind off 11(12, 14, 14, 14) stitches at the beginning of the next row, pattern 24(27, 30, 30, 30), turn. 25(28, 31, 31, 31) stitches on the needle

Row 1: P2tog, work in pattern to the end.

Row 2: Bind off 11(12, 14, 14, 14) stitches, work in pattern to the last 2 stitches, k2tog.

Row 3: P2tog, work in pattern to the end.

Row 4: Bind off the remaining stitches. Rejoin yarn to the remaining stitches with the right side of the work facing, bind off the central 48(48, 46, 48, 50) stitches, work in pattern to the end of the row.

Row 5: Bind off 11(12, 14, 14, 14) stitches, work in pattern to the end.

Row 6: Ssk, work in pattern to the end.

Row 7: Bind off 11(12, 14, 14, 14) stitches, work in pattern to the last 2 stitches, p2tog.

Row 8: Ssk, work in pattern to the end.

Row 9: Bind off the remaining stitches.

Sleeves

Cast on 56(56, 56, 60, 60) stitches using size 5 (3.75mm) needles. Work 19 rows in k2, p2 rib. Increase on the next (wrong side) row:

Small, Medium, and Large: (Rib 11, m1p) 4 times, end rib 12. 60(60, 60) stitches.

X-Large, XX-Large: (Rib 12, m1p) 4 times. 64(64) stitches.

Change to size 7 (4.5mm) needles and work in cable pattern as follows:

Row 1: (K1, p1) 1(1, 1, 2, 2) times, k1, k1tbl, p2, work row 1 of chart B, p2, k1tbl, work row 1 of chart A, k1tbl, p2, work row 1 of chart B, p2, k1tbl, k1, (p1, k1) 1(1, 1, 2, 2) times.

Row 2: (K1, p1) 1(1, 1, 2, 2) times, k1, p1tbl, k2, work row 2 of chart B, k2, p1tbl, work row 2 of chart A, p1tbl, k1, work row 2 of chart B, k2, p1tbl, k1, (p1, k1) 1(1, 1, 2, 2) times.

The 3(3, 3, 5, 5) stitches of seed stitch repeat each side of the cable pattern. Continue with patterns as set, increase 1 stitch at each end of rows as follows, taking increased stitches into the seed stitch panels:

Small, Medium, Large: On 9th and every following 8th row until there are 84(86, 90) stitches. Work even until the sleeve measures 19(19, 19¼)" (48[48, 49]cm) from the cast-on edge.

X-Large: On the 9th row, then * every following 8th, then 6th rows, repeat from * until there are 94 stitches. Work even until the sleeve measures 19 ¾" (50cm) from the cast-on edge.

XX-Large: On the 9th and every following 6th row until there are 100 stitches. Work even until the sleeve measures 20" (51cm) from the cast-on edge.

Shape sleeve cap

Small, Medium, and Large: Keeping the pattern correct, bind off 4 stitches at the beginning of the next 2 rows, then 3 stitches at the beginning of the following 2 rows, 2 stitches at the beginning of the following 14 rows, then 1 stitch at each end of every right-side row until 20(22, 22) stitches remain. Work 1 row even, bind off the remaining stitches.

X-Large: Keeping the pattern correct, bind off 4 stitches at the beginning of the next 4 rows, 3 stitches on the next 2 rows, and 2 stitches at the beginning of the following 12 rows, then 1 stitch at each end of every right-side row until 22 stitches remain. Work 1 row even, bind off the remaining stitches.

XX-Large: Keeping the pattern correct, bind off 4 stitches at the beginning of the next 4 rows, 3 stitches on the next 4 rows, and 2 stitches at the beginning of the next 10 rows. Decrease 1 stitch at each end of every right-side row until 24 stitches remain. Work 1 row even, bind off the remaining stitches.

Neckband

Sew right shoulder seam. With the right side of the work facing and using size 5 (3.75mm) needles, pick up and knit 24(24, 24, 26, 26) stitches down the left front neck, 14(14, 14, 14, 14) stitches across the center-front cast off stitches, 24(24, 24, 26, 26) stitches up the right front neck, and 50(50, 50, 50, 52) stitches across the back neck. 112(112, 112, 116, 118) stitches. Working in k2, p2 rib, work until the neckband is 3½" (9cm) deep. Bind off in rib.

Sew left shoulder seam, sew side seams, set in sleeves. Sew sleeve seams. Sew in all ends.

Chart A

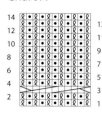

Chart B

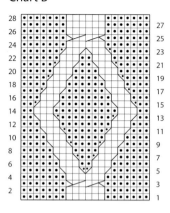

Chart C

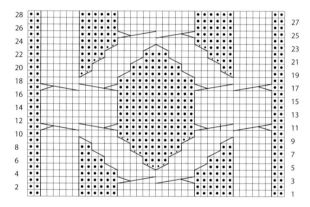

·   Purl on right side, knit on wrong side.

ℛ   Knit or purl through the back of the loop.

C4L; slip the next 3 stitches to a cable needle and hold at the front of the work, p1, k3 from the cable needle.

C4R; slip the next stitch to a cable needle and hold at the back of the work, k3, p1 from the cable needle

C6B; slip the next 3 stitches to a cable needle and hold at the back of the work, k3, k3 from the cable needle.

C8R; slip the next 2 stitches to a cable needle and hold at the back of the work, k6, p2 from the cable needle.

C8L; slip the next 6 stitches to a cable needle and hold at the front of the work, p2, k6 from the cable needle.

T11B; slip the next 6 stitches to a cable needle and hold at the back of the work, (k1b, p1, k1b, p1, k1b) over the next 5 stitches, (p1, k1b) 3 times from the cable needle.

C12F; slip the next 6 stitches to a cable needle and hold at the front of the work, k6, k6 from the cable needle.

C12B; slip the next 6 stitches to a cable needle and hold at the back of the work, k6, k6 from the cable needle.

Skill level: Experienced.

The leg section with the Argyle pattern is worked in intarsia, and as part rows / rounds back and forth on the needles rather than in complete rounds as is usual with socks. This prevents the colorwork from stranding across the interior of the sock, and the seams are formed where the colorwork diamonds are joined with the rest of the sock. The foot is worked in rounds.

Size: 17" (43cm) from top of ribbing to top of heel. Foot circumference: 9" (23cm).

Materials:
5 balls Rowan 4-ply Soft, 100% Wool [1¾oz (50g) 189yd (175m)], 3 in Nippy, 1 each of Honk and Whisper. **2** fine
Approximately 300 gunmetal gray glass beads ⅛" (3mm) in diameter.
2 yards (2m) of ⅜" (8mm) ribbon.
Set of 5 size 1 (2.5mm) double-pointed needles.

Gauge: 30 stitches and 40 rows to 4" (10cm) over stockinette stitch.

Cast on 108 stitches using Nippy and join into a round, taking care not to twist the stitches. Distribute evenly over 4 needles. Begin ribbing:

*K2, p1, repeat from * around for 1¾" (4.5cm).

Eyelet round: *K2, p1, yo, k2tog, p1, repeat from * around (you will have 18 eyelet holes).

Next round: Work even in k2, p1 rib as set until cuff measures 3¼" (8.5cm). Break yarn and thread 72 beads onto Nippy yarn at this point, and 13 beads onto Honk yarn. The beginning of the original ribbing round will be at the center front, rather than at the center back, as is more usual from now on.

Next part round / row: K2tog, k6, B1, k44, p1, k2, p1, k44, B1, k6. 107 stitches. Turn work.

Next part round / row: P51, k1, p2, k1, p51, turn work.

Next part round / row: With Honk, knit the last stitch as yet unworked from the previous row / part round. Twist Honk under Nippy yarn (the next stitch) to prevent a hole from forming, turn work, purl this stitch again in Honk. Turn work, drop Honk yarn. You have now completed 2 rounds / rows of the chart.

Next part round / row: Pick up Nippy yarn, k4, B1, pattern around to 6 stitches before the Honk stitch, B1, k4, slip last Nippy stitch from right hand needle to left hand needle with Honk stitch, turn work, twist yarn (to prevent a hole from forming).

Next part round / row: Pattern around (purl side of work facing) to 1 stitch before the Honk stitch, turn.

Next part round / row: With Honk, k3 (1 Nippy stitch either side of Honk stitch as set already), twist yarns, turn work.

Next part round / row: P3 with Honk, turn work.

You have now completed 4 rounds / rows of the chart.

Next part round / row: With Nippy, k2, B1, work in pattern to the last 4 stitches before the Honk stitches, B1, k2, slip last Nippy stitch to left-hand needle from right-hand needle (this is not essential, but it helps), twist yarns, turn work.

Next part round / row: Pattern around (purl side of work facing) to last Nippy stitch before the 3 Honk stitches, turn work.

Next part round / row: K5 Honk (1 stitch either side of 3 stitches as set), twist yarns, turn work.

Next part round / row: P5 Honk, twist yarns, turn work.

You have now completed 6 rounds / rows of chart.

Continue working this way, working 2 part rounds / rows in Nippy and then 2 in Honk (or Whisper, depending on which diamond you are knitting), placing beads as shown on the chart (do not forget to thread beads onto Whisper and Honk yarn before starting the other diamonds. You will need 13 on the two Whisper and the second Honk diamonds, and 9 on the last Honk diamond) and AT THE SAME TIME work decreases on the 10th row, then on every following 7th row 7 times, then on every following 5th row 15 times. Work decrease rows:

Work in pattern to 2 stitches before center back "p1, k2, p1," ssk, work p1, k2, p1 panel, k2 tog. After 137 rows of pattern you should have 5 diamonds complete and 61 stitches remaining on the needles. The last round will end at the point of the last (Honk) diamond (between what are needles # 1 & 2).

The stitches are now worked as follows: 31 for top of foot, held for the moment while the heel is worked, and 30 for the heel. Working on double-pointed needles this is 15 stitches on #1 needle (before the last diamond), 16 stitches on #2 needle (after the diamond) and 15 stitches each on needles 3 and 4 for heel.

Knit across the stitches on needle #2, begin heel.

Row 1: Sl1, k12, p1, k2, p1, k to end.

Row 2: Sl1, p12, k1, p2, k1, p to end.

Work these 2 rows 14 times more, 30 rows total.

Turn heel:

Row 1: Sl1, k15, k2tog, k1, turn.

Row 2: Sl1, p3, p2tog, p1, turn.

Row 3: Sl1, k4, k2tog, k1 turn.

Row 4: Sl1, p5, p2tog, p1 turn.

Continue this way, working 1 stitch more on each row until all stitches have been used up (last row will end "p2tog, p1"). 18 stitches remain on the needle.

Next round: Sl1, k across the 17 stitches remaining on what is now needle #1, pick up and knit 15 stitches along the side of the heel flap with this same needle.

Needles # 2 & 3 (top of foot): Knit across.

Needle # 4 (currently empty): Pick up and knit 15 stitches along the side of the heel flap, knit across the first 9 stitches from needle #1, round now begins at the mid-point of the heel and you have 79 stitches.

Round 1: K to last 2 stitches on #1, k2tog, k across the stitches on #2 and 3, ssk first 2 stitches on #4, knit to end.

Next round: Work even.

Repeat these 2 rounds until 61 stitches remain, then work in rounds of stockinette stitch until foot length is 7½" (19cm), or until foot is 2" (5cm) shorter than the foot the sock is for.

Toe shaping

Decrease round 1: *K2tog, k8, k2tog, k9, repeat from * around. 56 stitches. Work 5 rounds even.

Decrease round 2: *K2tog, k5, repeat from * around. 48 stitches. These decreases will not line up with the first round of the decreases as 8 stitches have been decreased on this round as opposed to 5 stitches on the previous decrease round. Work 4 rounds even.

Decrease round 3: *K2tog, k4, repeat from * around. 40 stitches. Work 3 rounds even.

Decrease round 4: *K2tog, k3, repeat from * around. 32 stitches. Work 2 rounds even.

Decrease round 5: *K2tog, k2, repeat from * around. 24 stitches. Work 1 round even.

Decrease round 6: *K2tog, k1, repeat from * around. 16 stitches.

Decrease round 7: *K2tog, repeat from * around. 8 stitches.

Finishing

Thread yarn through these 8 stitches, draw up and fasten off securely. Sew in all ends. Cut ribbon into two lengths and thread through eyelet holes.

☐ Nippy stitch

⊡ Nippy stitch with bead

■ Honk stitch

■ Honk stitch with bead

▨ Whisper stitch

⊙ Whisper stitch with bead

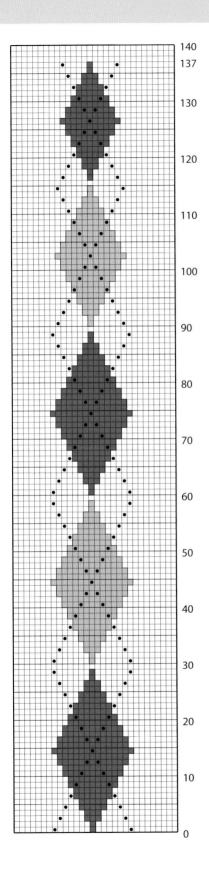

Strawberry Tea

FROM THE SOMERSET TEA BOUTIQUE

If you use loose tea: For a standard-size teapot, put in one teaspoon (5ml) of tea per person plus "one for the pot." (So if there are 4 of you having tea, use 5 teaspoons [25ml].)

Serves four to five

15 –20 medium-sized fresh strawberries

1 lemon

1 pint (480ml) vanilla ice cream

1 16-oz (454g) jar strawberry preserves

Put the tea in a teapot and fill the teapot with boiling water. Steep for 4 to 5 minutes or until the tea is the desired strength.

Hull the strawberries and cut in half lengthwise. Halve the lemon and squeeze the juice over the strawberries. Divide the strawberries among serving bowls.

Spoon vanilla ice cream on top of the strawberries. Spoon 1 tablespoon (15ml) of strawberry preserves on top of the ice cream.

Serve with the tea.

Somerset Tea Boutique

Radella
Nanu Oya
Dimbulla Valley
Sri Lanka

somersetestate@sltnet.lk

Dimbula Athletic & Cricket Club

Whether or not you are an avid cricket player, be sure to visit the grounds of the Dimbula Cricket Club to experience their stunning natural beauty. The adjoining Somerset Tea Boutique is a perfect spot to enjoy "Strawberry Tea" and a variety of other teas.

chapter three

GREEN TEA

Tea for two ... and a chance to catch up on a bit of gossip!

The setting is a historic summer house on the Tregothnan Tea Plantation, which forms part of the estate owned by the Boscawen family since 1335. The plantation produces the only black and green tea grown in England.

There are approximately 1,500 varieties of tea in the world, all offering different styles, taste, and color. The character of tea, like wine, is influenced by the elevation of the land, the soil, wind conditions, and temperature as well as the quality of the "plucking."

Although black tea is common in the United Kingdom, green tea is the most widely consumed drink in the world today, after water. This tea is made from the same plant as other teas—*Camellia sinensis*—but there is a process used that prevents oxidization.

The door to the garden of the Tregothnan Tea Estate.

Historically, a Buddhist priest in the Song Dynasty (who was also responsible for bringing the Rinzai School of Zen Buddhism to Japan) brought green tea to Japan from China.

In both China and Japan elaborate rituals were developed governing the preparation and drinking of tea. For formal tea ceremonies, the location, the vessels, and the stages of preparation of the drink have all been specified. Tea drinking in this context is supposed to provide an experience of grace and tranquility.

In terms of health benefits, green tea is said to be excellent for boosting the immune system. This tea is rich in antioxidants and is now consumed around the world as a preventive and cure for all sorts of ailments. Some people even use it to help with weight reduction.

Tregothnan green tea is brewed in a glass teapot and is drunk from matching glass cups. No sugar or milk should be added. Items to accompany the tea include Tregothnan clotted cream biscuits and multicolored cupcakes with a floral theme frosting.

Skill level: Intermediate.

Size: XS(S, M, L, XL, XXL).

Finished bust: 34(36, 40, 44, 48, 52)" (86[91, 101.5, 112, 122, 132]cm).

Materials:

10(11, 12, 12, 13, 14) balls RYC Cashsoft DK, Wool/ Microfiber/ Cashmere [1¾ oz (50g), 142yd (130m)], Lichen. **③** light

3 buttons, approximately ½" (13mm) diameter.

Size 3 (3.25mm) and 5 (3.75mm) needles.

Gauge: 24 stitches and 30 rows to 4" (10cm) over reverse stockinette stitch on size 5 (3.75mm) needles.

Back

Cast on 105(111, 123, 135, 147, 159) stitches using size 3 (3.25mm) needles and work 6 rows in seed stitch. Change to size 5 (3.75mm) needles and begin reverse stockinette stitch with a purl row. Work even for 10(10, 10, 12, 12, 12) rows, begin decreases:

First decrease row: Decrease 1 stitch at each end of the row, (p2, ssp, p to the last 4 stitches, p2tog, p2). *Work even for 7(7, 7, 9, 9, 9) rows, repeat the decrease row. Repeat from * once more. 99(105, 117, 129, 141, 153) stitches. Work even until the back measures 5¾(5¾, 5¾, 6, 6, 6)" (14.5[14.5, 14.5, 15, 15, 15]cm) from the cast-on edge, begin increases:

Increase row: Increase 1 stitch at each end of the row p2, m1p, p to the last 2 stitches, m1p, p2. * Work even for 7(7, 7, 9, 9, 9) rows, repeat the increase row. Repeat from * once more. 105(111, 123, 135, 147, 159) stitches. Work even until the back measures 13(13, 13½, 13½, 14, 14)" (33[33, 34.5, 34.5, 35.5, 35.5]cm) from the cast-on edge.

Begin the armhole decreases

X-Small and Small: Bind off 3 stitches at the beginning of the next 2 rows, then 2 stitches at the beginning of the following 2 rows. Bind off 1 stitch at the beginning of the next 10(12) rows. 85(89) stitches.

Medium and Large: Bind off 4 stitches at the beginning of the next 2 rows, then 3 stitches at the beginning of the following 2 rows, and 2 stitches at the beginning of the following 2(4) rows. Bind off 1 stitch at the beginning of the next 6(8) rows. 99(105) stitches.

X-Large and XX-Large: Bind off 4 stitches at the beginning of the next 2(4) rows, then 3 stitches at the beginning of the next 4 rows, and 2 stitches at the beginning of the following 4 rows. Bind off 1 stitch at the beginning of the following 8(12) rows. 109(111) stitches.

Work even until the armhole measures 2(2, 2½, 3, 3½, 3½)" (5[5, 6.5, 7.5, 9, 9]cm), begin flower motif:

Row 1: P42(44, 49, 52, 54, 55), k1tbl, p42(44, 49, 52, 54, 55).

Row 2: K42(44, 49, 52, 54, 55), p1, k42(44, 49, 52, 54, 55).

Work the remaining 28 rows of the flower motif from the chart as set, work even then until the armhole measures 7(7, 7½, 8, 8½, 9)" (18[18, 19, 20.5, 21.5, 23]cm). Shape shoulders and back neck.

Bind off 6(6, 8, 8, 8, 9) stitches at the beginning of the next 2 rows. Bind off 6(7, 8, 8, 9, 9) stitches at the beginning of the next row, p13(15, 17, 18, 19, 19) stitches (14[16, 18, 19, 20, 20] stitches just worked), turn.

Row 3: Bind off 1 stitch, knit to the end of the row.

Row 4: Bind off 6(7, 8, 8, 9, 9), purl to the end of the row.

Row 5: Bind off 1 stitch, knit to the end of the row.

Row 6: Bind off the remaining 6(7, 8, 9, 9, 9) stitches. With the right side of the work facing, rejoin yarn to the remaining stitches, bind off the central 33(31, 31, 35, 35, 35) stitches, purl to the end of the row.

Row 7: Bind off 6(7, 8, 8, 9, 9) stitches, knit to the end of the row.

Row 8: Bind off 1 stitch, purl to the end of the row.

Row 9: Bind off 6(7, 8, 8, 9, 9), knit to the end of the row.

Row 10: Bind off 1 stitch, purl to the end of the row.

Row 11: Bind off the remaining 6(7, 8, 9, 9, 9) stitches.

Left front

Cast on 57(61, 65, 71, 77, 83) stitches using size 3 (3.25mm) needles. Work 6 rows in seed stitch. Change to size 5 (3.75mm) needles and beginning reverse stockinette stitch, p53(57, 61, 67, 73, 79), turn. Leave the remaining 4 stitches on a holder for button band. Decrease 1 stitch at the beginning of the right-side rows

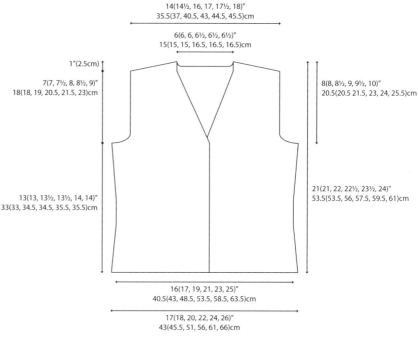

14(14½, 16, 17, 17½, 18)"
35.5(37, 40.5, 43, 44.5, 45.5)cm

6(6, 6, 6½, 6½, 6½)"
15(15, 15, 16.5, 16.5, 16.5)cm

1"(2.5cm)

7(7, 7½, 8, 8½, 9)"
18(18, 19, 20.5, 21.5, 23)cm

8(8, 8½, 9, 9½, 10)"
20.5(20.5 21.5, 23, 24, 25.5)cm

13(13, 13½, 13½, 14, 14)"
33(33, 34.5, 34.5, 35.5, 35.5)cm

21(21, 22, 22½, 23½, 24)"
53.5(53.5, 56, 57.5, 59.5, 61)cm

16(17, 19, 21, 23, 25)"
40.5(43, 48.5, 53.5, 58.5, 63.5)cm

17(18, 20, 22, 24, 26)"
43(45.5, 51, 56, 61, 66)cm

(side edge—p2, ssp, p to end) as for the back on the 11th(11th, 11th, 13th, 13th, 13th) row and the following 7th(7th, 7th, 9th, 9th, 9th) row twice. When the front measures 4½(4½, 4¾, 4¾, 5, 5)" (11.5(11.5, 12, 12, 12.5, 12.5]cm), begin the fork motif:

Fork motif row 1: P21(23, 25, 28, 31, 34), m1k, inc-k, p5, m1k, p5, inc-k, m1k p to end.

Fork motif row 2 (and all wrong-side rows until the Row 20): Work stitches as they face you.

This places the fork motif, work the remaining 40 rows as shown on the chart, and AT THE SAME TIME, begin increases at the beginning of the right-side rows (side edge—p2, m1p, p to end) when the front measures 5¾(5¾, 5¾, 6, 6, 6)" (14.5[14.5, 14.5, 15, 15, 15]cm) from the cast-on edge. *Work even for 7(7, 7, 9, 9, 9) rows, repeat the increase row, repeat from * once more.

Work even until the front measures 13(13, 13½, 13½, 14, 14)" (33[33, 34.5, 34.5, 35.5, 35.5]cm) from the cast-on edge.

Begin the armhole and neck decreases

Next row: Bind off 3(3, 4, 4, 4, 4) stitches at the beginning of the row, p to the end of the row.

Next row: Decrease 1 stitch at the beginning of this row (k1, ssk, k to end), and repeat this decrease on the next 11 wrong-side rows. AT THE SAME TIME, continue the armhole shaping at the beginning of the right-side rows, bind off 2(2, 3, 3, 3, 4) stitches on the next right-side row, 1(1, 2, 2, 3, 3) on the next, 1(1, 1, 2, 2, 3) on the next, 1(1, 1, 1, 2, 2) on the next, 1(1, 1, 1, 1, 2) on the next, and 1 on the next 1(2, 0, 2, 3, 6) right-side rows.

After 12 decreases worked in total at the neck edge, decrease 1 stitch at the neck edge on every other wrong-side row (every 4th row) 7(7, 5, 7, 7, 7) times. 24(27, 32, 33, 35, 36) stitches. Work even until front armhole matches back armhole to the beginning of the shoulder shaping, 7(7, 7½, 8, 8½, 9)" (18[18, 19, 20.5, 21.5, 23]cm).

Begin shoulder shaping

Next row (right side): Bind off 6(6, 8, 8, 8, 9) stitches at the beginning of the row.

Next row: Work even.

Next 2 right-side rows: Bind off 6(7, 8, 8, 9, 9) stitches at the beginning of the rows.

Next row: Work even.

Next row: Bind off the remaining 6(7, 8, 9, 9, 9) stitches.

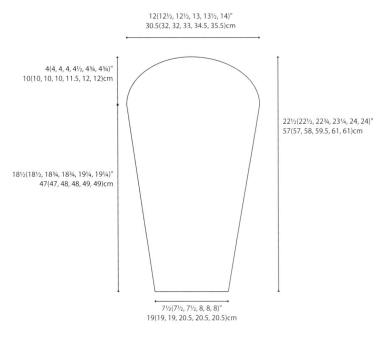

12(12½, 12½, 13, 13½, 14)"
30.5(32, 32, 33, 34.5, 35.5)cm

4(4, 4, 4, 4½, 4¾, 4¾)"
10(10, 10, 10, 11.5, 12, 12)cm

22½(22½, 22¾, 23¼, 24, 24)"
57(57, 58, 59.5, 61, 61)cm

18½(18½, 18¾, 18¾, 19¼, 19¼)"
47(47, 48, 48, 49, 49)cm

7½(7½, 7½, 8, 8, 8)"
19(19, 19, 20.5, 20.5, 20.5)cm

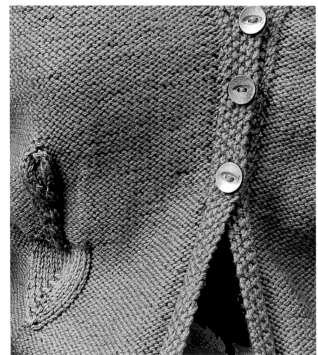

Right front

Cast on 57(61, 65, 71, 77, 83) stitches using size 3 (3.25mm) needles. Work 6 rows in seed stitch.

Next row: Seed stitch 4, slip these stitches onto a holder for the buttonhole band, change to size 5 (3.75mm) needles and p53(57, 61, 67, 73, 79). Decrease 1 stitch at the end of the right-side rows (side edge—purl to the last 4 stitches, p2tog, p2) as for the back on the 11th(11th, 11th, 13th, 13th, 13th) row and the following 7th(7th, 7th, 9th, 9th, 9th) row twice. When the front measures 4½(4½, 4¾, 4¾, 5, 5)" (11.5(11.5, 12, 12, 12.5, 12.5]cm), begin the trowel motif:

Trowel motif

Motif row 1: P24 (26, 28, 31, 33, 36), CDI, p to end of row.

Row 2: Work stitches as they face you, as shown on the Trowel Motif chart.

This places the trowel motif, work the remaining 40 rows as shown on the Trowel Motif chart, and AT THE SAME TIME, begin increases at the end of the right-side rows (side edge—purl to the last 2 stitches, m1p, purl to end) when the front measures 5¾(5¾, 5¾, 6, 6, 6)" (14.5[14.5, 14.5, 15, 15, 15]cm) from the cast-on edge. *Work even for 7(7, 7, 9, 9, 9) rows, repeat the increase row, repeat from * once more.

Work even until the front measures 13(13, 13½, 13½, 14, 14)" (33[33, 34.5, 34.5, 35.5, 35.5]cm) from the cast-on edge with the wrong side of the work facing. Begin the armhole and neck decreases:

First decrease row: Bind off 3(3, 4, 4, 4, 4) stitches at the beginning of the row, p to the end of the row.

Second decrease row: Decrease 1 stitch at the beginning of this row (p1, ssp, p to end), and repeat this decrease on the next 11 right-side rows. AT THE SAME TIME, continue the armhole shaping at the beginning of the wrong-side rows, bind off 2(2, 3, 3, 3, 4) stitches on the next wrong-side row, 1(1, 2, 2, 3, 3) on the next, 1(1, 1, 2, 2, 3) on the next, 1(1, 1, 1, 2, 2) on the next, 1(1, 1, 1, 1, 2) on the next, and 1 on the next 1(2, 0, 2, 3, 6) wrong-side rows.

After 12 decreases worked in total at the neck edge, decrease 1 stitch at the neck edge on every other right-side row (every 4th row) 7(7, 5, 7, 7, 7) times. 24(27, 32, 33, 35, 36) stitches. Work even until the front armhole matches the back armhole to the beginning of the shoulder shaping, 7(7, 7½, 8, 8½, 9)" (18[18, 19, 20.5, 21.5, 23]cm), with the wrong side of the work facing. Begin shoulder shaping:

Next row (wrong side): Bind off 6(6, 8, 8, 8, 9) stitches at the beginning of the row.

Next row: Work even.

Next 2 wrong-side rows: Bind off 6(7, 8, 8, 9, 9) stitches at the beginning of the rows.

Next row: Work even.

Next row: Bind off the remaining 6(7, 8, 9, 9, 9) stitches.

Buttonband

Join the shoulder seams. With the right side of the left front facing, slip held stitches onto a size 3 (3.25mm) needle. Rejoin yarn, kfb in the first stitch, work in seed stitch to the end of the row. 5 stitches. Work even in seed stitch keeping the made stitch in stockinette stitch for ease of sewing up. Work until band fits to the beginning of the neck shaping when slightly stretched. Mark 3 button positions, the first to come 1" (2.5cm) down from the beginning of the neck shaping, the next to come 1½" (3.8cm) below that, and the next to come 1½" (3.8cm) below this one. When the band reaches to the beginning of the neck shaping, begin increases on the inside (side to join to the front) of the band. With the right side of the front (and therefore the band) facing, k1, m1, work in pattern to the end. Keep the inside edge stitch in stockinette stitch (as before), and increase on right-side rows (every alternate row) 9 times (14 stitches) and then on every 4th row 5 times until there are 19 stitches. Now work even until the collar reaches to 1" (2.5cm) below the

shoulder seam without stretching, and with the wrong side of the collar facing (in other words, the outside edge of the collar is the beginning of the row).

Next row: Work in pattern to the last 8 stitches, wt.

Next row: Work in pattern to the end of the row.

Next 2 rows: Work all stitches, working wrap with wrapped stitch.

Repeat these 4 rows until the collar reaches the center-back of the back neck without stretching, bind off in seed stitch.

Buttonhole band

With the wrong side of the right front facing, slip held stitches onto a size 3 (3.25mm) needle. Rejoin yarn, kfb in the first stitch, work in seed stitch to the end of the row. Work even in seed stitch (keeping the made stitch in stockinette stitch for ease of sewing up), until buttonhole band reaches the point of the first marked button on the left front, with the right side of the work facing. Make buttonhole:

Garden Jacket Trowel Motif chart

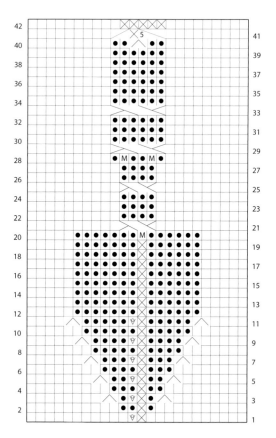

Garden Jacket Flower Motif chart

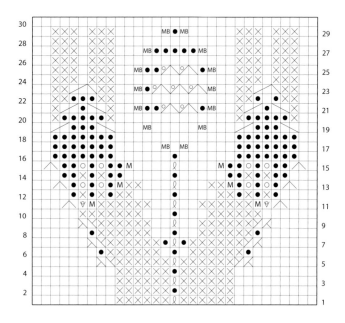

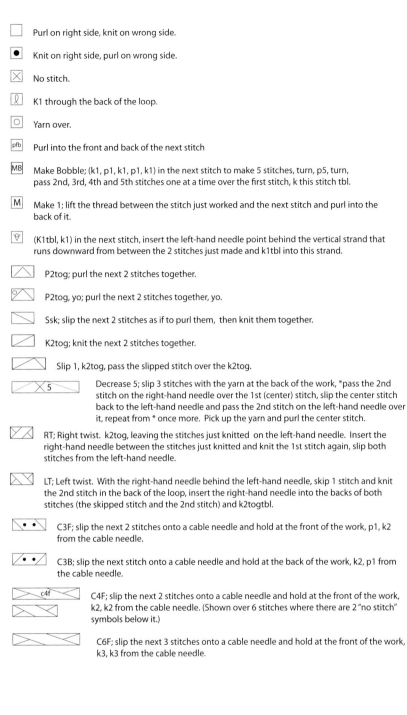

Purl on right side, knit on wrong side.

Knit on right side, purl on wrong side.

No stitch.

K1 through the back of the loop.

Yarn over.

pfb Purl into the front and back of the next stitch

MB Make Bobble; (k1, p1, k1, p1, k1) in the next stitch to make 5 stitches, turn, p5, turn, pass 2nd, 3rd, 4th and 5th stitches one at a time over the first stitch, k this stitch tbl.

M Make 1; lift the thread between the stitch just worked and the next stitch and purl into the back of it.

(K1tbl, k1) in the next stitch, insert the left-hand needle point behind the vertical strand that runs downward from between the 2 stitches just made and k1tbl into this strand.

P2tog; purl the next 2 stitches together.

P2tog, yo; purl the next 2 stitches together, yo.

Ssk; slip the next 2 stitches as if to purl them, then knit them together.

K2tog; knit the next 2 stitches together.

Slip 1, k2tog, pass the slipped stitch over the k2tog.

5 Decrease 5; slip 3 stitches with the yarn at the back of the work, *pass the 2nd stitch on the right-hand needle over the 1st (center) stitch, slip the center stitch back to the left-hand needle and pass the 2nd stitch on the left-hand needle over it, repeat from * once more. Pick up the yarn and purl the center stitch.

RT; Right twist. k2tog, leaving the stitches just knitted on the left-hand needle. Insert the right-hand needle between the stitches just knitted and knit the 1st stitch again, slip both stitches from the left-hand needle.

LT; Left twist. With the right-hand needle behind the left-hand needle, skip 1 stitch and knit the 2nd stitch in the back of the loop, insert the right-hand needle into the backs of both stitches (the skipped stitch and the 2nd stitch) and k2togtbl.

C3F; slip the next 2 stitches onto a cable needle and hold at the front of the work, p1, k2 from the cable needle.

C3B; slip the next stitch onto a cable needle and hold at the back of the work, k2, p1 from the cable needle.

c4f C4F; slip the next 2 stitches onto a cable needle and hold at the front of the work, k2, k2 from the cable needle. (Shown over 6 stitches where there are 2 "no stitch" symbols below it.)

C6F; slip the next 3 stitches onto a cable needle and hold at the front of the work, k3, k3 from the cable needle.

Garden Jacket Fork Motif chart

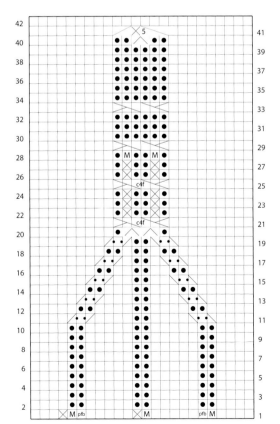

Seed stitch 2, yo, k2tog, work the last stitch. Work even until the buttonhole band is as long as button band, working 2 more buttonholes where marked.

When the band reaches to the beginning of the neck shaping, begin increases on the inside (side to join to the front) of the band. With the wrong side of the front (and therefore the band) facing, k1, m1, work in pattern to the end. Keep the inside edge stitch in stockinette stitch (as before), and increase on the wrong-side rows (every alternate row) 9 times (14 stitches) and then on every 4th row 5 times until there are 19 stitches. Now work even until the collar reaches to 1" (2.5cm) below the shoulder seam without stretching, and with the right side of the collar facing (in other words, the inside edge of the collar is the beginning of the row).

Next row: Work in pattern to the last 8 stitches, wt.

Next row: Work in pattern to the end of the row.

Next 2 rows: Work all stitches, working wrap with wrapped stitch.

Repeat these 4 rows until the collar reaches the center-back of the back neck without stretching, bind off in seed stitch.

Pockets

Cast on 7 stitches using size 5 (3.75mm) needles and purl 1 row.

Next row: K1, m1, k3, m1, k1. 9 stitches.

Next row (and every right-side row): Purl.

Next row: K1, m1, k1, m1, k3, m1, k1, m1, k1. 13 stitches.

Next increase row: K1, m1, k9, m1, k1. 15 stitches.

Next increase row: K1, m1, k1, m1, k9, m1, k1, m1, k1. 19 stitches.

Next increase row: K1, m1, k1m, m1, k11, m1, k1m, m1, k1. 24 stitches.

Beginning with a purl row, work 10 rows in reverse stockinette stitch. Change to size 3 (3.25mm), work 4 rows in seed stitch, bind off.

Sew pockets to fronts as shown in the photograph, below the fork and trowel motifs.

Sleeves

Cast on 46(46, 46, 50, 50, 50) stitches using size 3 (3.25mm) needles. Work 5 rows in seed stitch:

Next row: Pattern 3(3, 3, 5, 5, 5), m1, *pattern 10, m1, repeat from * to the last 3(3, 3, 5, 5, 5) stitches, work in pattern to the end of the row. 51(51, 51, 55, 55, 55) stitches.

Change to size 5 (3.75mm) needles and begin reverse stockinette stitch and twisted rib pattern:

Next row: P3(3, 3, 5, 5, 5), *k1tbl, p10, rep from * 3 times more, k1tbl, p3(3, 3, 5, 5, 5).

All wrong-side rows: Work stitches as they face you. Work increases as follows:

X-Small: Increase 1 stitch (p2, m1p, p to the last 2 stitches, m1p, p2) at each end of the 9th and every following 10th row until there are 77 stitches, work even until the sleeve measures 18½" (47cm) from the cast-on edge.

Small, Medium, Large: Increase 1 stitch (p2, m1p, p to the last 2 stitches, m1p, p2) at each end of the 9th and every following 8th row until there are 81(81, 83) stitches, work even until the sleeve measures 18½(18¾, 18¾)" (47[48, 48]cm) from the cast-on edge.

X-Large, XX-Large: Increase 1 stitch (p2, m1p, p to the last 2 stitches, m1p, p2) at each end of the 9th and every following *6th, then every following 8th row, repeat from * until there are 87(91) stitches, work even until the sleeve measures 19¼(19¼)" (49[49]cm) from the cast-on edge.

Shape sleeve cap

Bind off 3 stitches at the beginning of the next 2(2, 2, 4, 4, 4) rows, then 2 stitches at the beginning of the following 2(2, 2, 4, 6, 6) rows. Decrease 1 stitch at each end of the next 7 right-side rows, then bind off 2 stitches at the beginning of the next 14(14, 14, 12, 12, 12) rows. Bind off the remaining stitches.

Finishing

Set in sleeves, sew sleeve and side seams. Sew in all ends. Sew on buttons.

SUMMER HOUSE SWEATER

Skill Level: Intermediate

Size: XS(S, M, L, XL, XXL).

Finished bust: 32½(36½, 40½, 44½, 48½, 52½)" (82.5[93, 103, 113, 123, 133]cm).

Materials:
7(8, 8, 9, 9, 10) balls Karabella Yarns Lace Merino, 100% Merino Wool [1¾ oz (50g), 255yd (235m)], Silver. (●●) lace
Approximately 2,250(2,500, 3,000, 3,000, 3,000, 3,500) ¼"(6mm) flat white sequins.
Size 2 (2.75mm) and size 3(3.25mm) needles.

Gauge: 44 rows and 30 stitches to 4" (10cm) over stockinette stitch in size 3(3.25mm) needles.

Back

Cast on 107(125, 137, 155, 171, 187) stitches with size 2 (2.75mm) needles. Work 11 rows in seed stitch. Break yarn, thread on sequins, change to size 3 (3.25mm) needles and work in pattern:

Foundation row (wrong side): (K1, p1) 1(3, 3, 8, 12, 13) times, k1 0(0, 1, 0, 0, 1) time, p103(113, 123, 123, 123, 133), (k1, p1) 1(3, 3, 8, 12, 13) times, k1 0(0, 1, 0, 0, 1) time.

Row 1: (K1, p1) 1(3, 3, 8, 12, 13) times, k1 0(0, 1, 0, 0, 1) time, k1* yo, ssk, k1, k1tbl, SQ1, k1, SQ1, k1tbl, k2, repeat from * to the last 4(8, 9, 18, 26, 29) stitches, yo, ssk, (k1, p1) 1(3, 3, 8, 12, 13) times, k1 0(0, 1, 0, 0, 1) time.

Row 2 and all wrong-side rows: As the foundation row. The 2(6, 7, 16, 24, 27) stitch panels of seed stitch repeat at each end of the rows from now on, and are not repeated in the following instructions:

Row 3: K2 *yo, ssk, k1, k1tbl, SQ1, k1tbl, k1, k2tog, yo, k1* repeat from * 9(10, 11, 11, 11, 12) times more, end k1.

Row 5: K3 *yo, ssk, k1, k1tbl, k1, k2tog, yo, k3, repeat from * 9(10, 11, 11, 11, 12) times more.

Row 7: K1 *SQ1, k2, yo, ssk, k1, k2tog, yo, k2, repeat from * 9(10, 11, 11, 11, 12) times more, end SQ1, k1.

Row 9: K1, k1tbl, *SQ1, k2, yo, sl1, k2tog, psso, yo, k2, SQ1, k1tbl, repeat from * 9(10, 11, 11, 11, 12) times more, end k1.

Row 11: K2 *k1tbl, SQ1, k5, SQ1, k1tbl, k1, repeat from * 9(10, 11, 11, 11, 12) times more, end k1tbl.

Row 13: *K3, k1tbl, SQ1, k3, SQ1, k1tbl, repeat from * 9(10, 11, 11, 11, 12) times more, end k3.

These rows set the chevron sequin pattern. Work increases as follows:

X-Small, Small: Increase 1 stitch at each end (kfb, work in pattern to the last stitch, kfb) of the 11th and every following 10th row until there are 125(143) stitches**. Work even until the back measures 14½(15)" (37[38]cm), ending with the right side facing for the next row.

Medium, Large, X-Large: Increase 1 stitch at each end (kfb, work in pattern to the last stitch, kfb) of the 13th and every following 14th row until there are 155(173, 189) stitches**. Work even until the back measures 15(15½, 15½)" (38[39, 39]cm), ending with the right side facing for the next row.

XX-Large: Increase 1 stitch at each end (kfb, work in pattern to the last stitch, kfb) of the 13th and every following 16th row until there are 205 stitches**. Work even until the back measures 15¾" (40cm), ending with the right side facing for the next row.

X-Small: Bind off 3 stitches at the beginning of the next 2 rows, then 2 stitches at the beginning of the following 4 rows. 111 stitches. Work even until the armhole measures 7¾" (20cm).

Small, Medium: Bind off 6 stitches at the beginning of the next 2 rows, 4 stitches at the beginning of the next 2 rows, and 2 stitches at the beginning of the following 2 rows. Decrease 1 stitch at each end of the next 3(2) right-side rows. 113(127) stitches. Work even until the armhole measures 8¼(8¼)" (21[21]cm).

Large: Bind off 6 stitches at the beginning of the next 2 rows, then 4 at the beginning of the next 2, 3 stitches at the beginning of the next 2, and 2 stitches at the beginning of the next 4 rows. Decrease 1 stitch at each end of the next 2 right-side rows. 135 stitches. Work even until the armhole measures 8½" (21.5cm).

X-Large, XX-Large: Bind off 6 stitches at the beginning of the next 2 rows, 5 stitches at the beginning of the following 2 rows, and 4 stitches at the beginning of

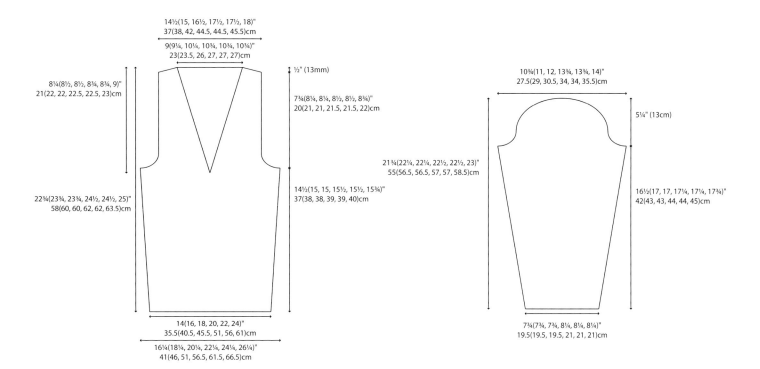

14½(15, 16½, 17½, 17½, 18)"
37(38, 42, 44.5, 44.5, 45.5)cm

9(9¼, 10¼, 10¾, 10¾, 10¾)"
23(23.5, 26, 27, 27, 27)cm

8¼(8½, 8½, 8¾, 8¾, 9)"
21(22, 22, 22.5, 22.5, 23)cm

½" (13mm)

7¾(8¼, 8¼, 8½, 8½, 8¾)"
20(21, 21, 21.5, 21.5, 22)cm

22¾(23¾, 23¾, 24½, 24½, 25)"
58(60, 60, 62, 62, 63.5)cm

14½(15, 15, 15½, 15½, 15¾)"
37(38, 38, 39, 39, 40)cm

14(16, 18, 20, 22, 24)"
35.5(40.5, 45.5, 51, 56, 61)cm

16¼(18¼, 20¼, 22¼, 24¼, 26¼)"
41(46, 51, 56.5, 61.5, 66.5)cm

10¾(11, 12, 13¾, 13¾, 14)"
27.5(29, 30.5, 34, 34, 35.5)cm

5¼" (13cm)

21¾(22¼, 22¼, 22½, 22½, 23)"
55(56.5, 56.5, 57, 57, 58.5)cm

16½(17, 17, 17¼, 17¼, 17¾)"
42(43, 43, 44, 44, 45)cm

7¾(7¾, 7¾, 8¼, 8¼, 8¼)"
19.5(19.5, 19.5, 21, 21, 21)cm

the next 2 rows. Bind off 3 stitches at the beginning of the next 2(4) rows, and 2 stitches on the next 6(6) rows. Decrease 1 stitch at each end of the next 3(7) right-side rows. 135(137) stitches. Work even until the armhole measures 8½(8¾)" (21.5[22]cm).

Shape shoulders. Bind off 7(7, 8, 9, 9, 9) stitches at the beginning of the next 2 rows.

Next row: Bind off 7(7, 8, 9, 9, 9) stitches, pattern 7(7, 8, 9, 9, 9). 8(8, 9, 10, 10, 10) stitches on the right-hand needle, turn.

Next row: P2tog, work in pattern to the end.

Next row: Bind off the remaining 7(7, 8, 9, 9, 9) stitches. Slip the central 67(69, 67, 77, 79, 81) stitches onto a holder for the back neck, rejoin yarn to the remaining stitches and work in pattern to the end.

Next row: Bind off 7(7, 8, 9, 9, 9) stitches, work in pattern to the end.

Next row: Ssk, work in pattern to the end.

Next row: Bind off the remaining 7(7, 8, 9, 9, 9) stitches.

Front

Work as for back to **. Work until length from cast-on edge is 14¼(14½, 14½, 15, 15, 15¼)" (36[37, 37, 38, 38, 39]cm), ending with the right side facing for the next row. Divide for neck shaping:

Next row: Pattern 62(71, 77, 86, 94, 102), turn. Work on these stitches only for the left front neck.

Next row: Keeping the pattern correct, work in pattern to the last 2 stitches, k2tog.

Next row: Work even.

X-Small, Small: Decrease at the neck edge on the next row, *then on the following 3rd row, work 1 row even and decrease on the next row, repeat from *. AT THE SAME TIME, when the side edge of the left front measures 14½(15)" (37[38]cm) with the right side of the work facing, begin armhole decreases. Bind off 3(6) stitches on this row, then 2(4) stitches on the next right-side row, 2(2) stitches on the next right-side row, and then decrease 1 stitch at the armhole edge on the next 0(3) right-side rows. Continue with the neck decreases as set until 21(21) stitches remain, work even until the armhole measures 7¾(8¼)" (20[21]cm). Bind off 7(7) stitches at the beginning of the next 3 right-side rows.

Medium, Large, X-Large, XX-Large: Decrease 1 stitch at the neck edge on the next and every other row 13(13, 14, 14) times, then decrease on the following *3rd row, work 1 row even and decrease on the next row, repeat from *. At the same time when the side edge on the left front measures 15(15½, 15½, 15¾)" (38[39, 39, 40]cm), with the right side of the work facing, begin armhole decreases. Bind off 6(6, 6, 6) stitches at the beginning of the next row, 4(4, 5, 5) at the beginning of the next right-side row and 2(3, 4, 4) on the next right-side row. Bind off 1(2, 3, 3) stitches on the next right-side row, then 1(2, 2, 3) stitches on the following right-side row. Armhole decreases are now finished for the medium size, work even until the armhole measures 8¼" (21cm). The following decreases are for the Large, X-Large, and XX-Large sizes only.

Large: Decrease 1 stitch at the beginning of the next 2 right-side rows only, work even until the armhole measures 8½" (21.5cm).

X-Large, XX-Large: Bind off 2(2) stitches on the next 2(3) right-side rows, then 1 stitch on the following 3(7) right-side rows. Work even until the armhole measures 8½(8¾)" (21.5[22]cm).

Shape shoulders

Bind off 8(9, 9, 9) stitches at the beginning of the next 3 right-side rows. Place central stitch from the front onto a holder for the neckband, rejoin yarn to the remaining 62(71, 77, 86, 94, 102) stitches, work in pattern to the end.

Next row: Keeping the pattern correct, work in pattern to the last 2 stitches, p2tog. Next row: Work even.

X-Small, Small: Decrease at the neck edge on the next row, *then on the following 3rd row, work 1 row even and decrease on the next row, repeat from *. AT THE SAME TIME, when the side edge of the right front measures 14½(15)" (37[38]cm) with the wrong side of the work facing, begin armhole decreases. Bind off 3(6) stitches on this row, then 2(4) stitches on the next wrong-side row, 2(2) stitches on the next wrong-side row, and then decrease 1 stitch at the armhole edge on the next 0(3) right-side rows. Continue with the neck decreases as set until 21(21) stitches remain, work even until the armhole measures 7¾(8¼)" (20[21]cm). Bind off 7(7) stitches at the beginning of the next 3 wrong-side rows.

Medium, Large, X-Large, XX-Large: Decrease 1 stitch at the neck edge on the next and every other row 13(13, 14, 14) times, then decrease on the following *3rd row, work 1 row even and decrease on the next row, repeat from *. At the same time when the side edge on the right front measures 15(15½, 15½,15¾)" (38[39, 39, 40]cm), with the wrong side of the work facing, begin armhole decreases. Bind off 6(6, 6, 6) stitches at the beginning of the next row, 4(4, 5, 5) at the beginning of the next wrong-side row, and 2(3, 4, 4) on the next wrong-side row. Bind off 1(2, 3, 3) stitches on the next wrong-side row, then 1(2, 2, 3) stitches on the following wrong-side row. Armhole decreases are now finished for the medium size, work even until the armhole measures 8¼" (21cm). The following decreases are for the Large, X-Large, and XX-Large sizes only.

Large: Decrease 1 stitch at the beginning of the next 2 wrong-side rows only, work even until the armhole measures 8½" (21.5cm).

X-Large, XX-Large: Bind off 2(2) stitches on the next 2(3) wrong-side rows, then 1 stitch on the following 3(7) wrong-side rows. Work even until the armhole measures 8½(8¾)" (21.5[22]cm).

Shape shoulders

Bind off 8(9, 9, 9) stitches at the beginning of the next 3 wrong-side rows.

Sleeves

Cast on 59(59, 59, 63, 63, 63) stitches using size 2 (2.75mm) needles. Work in seed stitch for 11 rows.

Row 12: P18(18, 18, 20, 20, 20), m1p, p2, m1p, p19, m1p, p2, m1p, p18(18, 18, 20, 20, 20). 63(63, 63, 67, 67, 67) stitches.

Break yarn, thread on sequins, change to size 3 (2.75mm) needles, continue in chevron sequin and lace cable pattern as follows:

Row 1: (K1, p1) 0(0, 0, 1, 1, 1) time, *k4, k1tbl, k3, SQ1, k3, k1tbl, k4, **p1, k2, yo, k2tog, p1*** repeat from * to ***, then from * to **, end (p1, k1) 0(0, 0, 1, 1, 1) time.

Row 2 (and every following wrong-side row): (K1, p1) 0(0, 0, 1, 1, 1) time, *p17, **k1, p2, yrn, p2tog, k1***, rep from * to ***, then from * to **, (p1, k1) 0(0, 0, 1, 1, 1) time. The Large, X-Large, and XX-Large sizes have 2 stitches in seed stitch that repeat at each edge of the work, these stitches are not written out in the following pattern rows:

Row 3: *K7, SQ1, k1b, k7, **p1, k2, yo, k2tog, p1*** repeat from * to ***, then from * to **.

Row 5: *K6, SQ1, k1tbl, k1, k1tbl, SQ1, k6, **p1, k2, yo, k2tog, p1***, repeat from * to *** then from * to **.

Row 7: *K5, SQ1, k1tbl, k3, k1tbl, SQ1, k5, **p1, k2, yo, k2tog, p1***, repeat from * to ***, then from * to **.

Row 9: *K4, SQ1, k1tbl, k5, k1tbl, SQ1, k4, **p1, c4f, p1***, repeat from * to ***, then from * to **.

Row 10: As 2nd.

Repeat these 10 rows and at the same time increase 1 stitch (kfb, work in pattern to the last stitch, kfb) at each end of the following rows, taking the increased stitches into panels of seed stitch:

X-Small: Increase on the 13th and every following 14th row until there are 83 stitches. Work even until the sleeve measures 16½" (42cm) from the cast-on edge.

Small, Medium: Increase on the 13th and every following 12th row until there are 87(91) stitches. Work even until the sleeve measures 17(17)" ([43, 43]cm) from the cast-on edge.

Large, X-Large: Increase on the 9th and every following 10th row until there are 103(103) stitches. Work even until the sleeve measures 17¼(17¼)" (44[44]cm) from the cast-on edge.

XX-Large: Increase on the 9th and every following 8th row until there are 107 stitches. Work even until the sleeve measures 17¾" (45cm) from the cast-on edge.

Shape sleeve cap

X-Small, Medium: Keeping the pattern correct, bind off 3(6) stitches at the beginning of the next 2 rows, 0(4) stitches at the beginning of the next 0(2) rows, then 2 stitches at the beginning of the following 2 rows, then 1 stitch at each end of the next 8 right-side rows. Work 3 rows even, * decrease 1 stitch at each end of the next right-side row, work 3 rows even, repeat from * twice more. Decrease 1 stitch at each end of the next 3 right-side rows, bind off 2 stitches at the beginning of the next 14 rows. Bind off the remaining 9 stitches.

Small: Bind off 6 stitches at the beginning of the next 2 rows, then 4 stitches at the beginning of the next 2, and 2 stitches at the beginning of the following 2 rows. Decrease 1 stitch at each end of the next 4 rows, *work 3 rows even, decrease 1 stitch at each end of the next row, repeat from * 4 times more. Decrease 1 stitch at each end of the next 3 right-side rows, the 2 stitches at the beginning of the next 14 rows. Bind off the remaining 9 stitches.

Large, X-Large, XX-Large: Bind off 6 stitches at the beginning of the next 2 rows, then 4 stitches at the beginning of the following 2 rows, then 3 stitches at the beginning of the next 2 rows. Bind off 2 stitches at the beginning of the next 4 rows, decrease 1 stitch at each end of the next 4 right-side rows. * Work 3 rows even, decrease 1 stitch at each end of the next row, repeat from * 4 times more. Decrease 1 stitch at each end of the following 3 right-side rows, bind off 2 stitches

at the beginning of the next 14 right-side rows. Bind off the remaining 17(21) stitches.

Neckband

Join the right shoulder seam. With the right side of the work facing and size 2 (2.75mm) needles, pick up and knit 71(75, 75, 79, 79, 81) stitches down the left side of the front neck, mark and knit the stitch held at the center-front neck, pick up and knit 71(75, 75, 79, 79, 81) stitches up the right side of the front neck, and knit across the 67(69, 67, 77, 79, 81) stitches from the back neck. 210(220, 218, 236, 238, 244) stitches. Beginning k1, work in seed stitch down to 2 stitches before the marked stitch, ssk, purl the marked stitch, k2tog, continue in seed stitch to the end of the row. Work 1 row even. Work these 2 rows 4 times more. 200(210, 208, 226, 228, 234) stitches. Bind off in seed stitch.

Finishing

Set in sleeves, sew side and sleeve seams, sew in all ends.

Skill level: Easy.

Size: To fit a teapot of 19" (48.5cm) circumference.

Pom-pom Tea Cozy

Materials:

2 balls RYC Cashsoft 4 ply, 57% Extra Fine Merino Wool, 33% Microfiber, 10% Cashmere [1¾ oz (50g), 197yd (180m)], 1 each of Redwood and Amethyst. **(2)** fine

Approximately 200 1" (2.5cm) diameter pink sequins.

Size 5 (3.75mm) needles, size 5F (3.75mm) crochet hook.

Gauge: 22 stitches and 44 rows to 4"(10cm) in garter stitch on size 5 needles.

Sparkle Tea Cozy

Materials:

4 spools Lion Brand Lamé, 65% Rayon, 35% Metalized Polyester [0.67 oz (19g), 75yd (67m)], in Silver. **(1)** super fine

Approximately 250 ½" (13mm) silver sequins and 12 1" (2.5cm) diameter silver sequins.

Thin beading wire.

Size 5 (3.75mm) needles, size 5F (3.75mm) crochet hook.

Gauge: 22 stitches and 44 rows to 4" (10cm) in garter stitch on size 5 needles.

Pom-pom Tea Cozy

Work in 12 row stripes of Redwood and Amethyst throughout.

Cast on 96 stitches using Redwood and work in garter stitch stripe pattern for 2¼" (5.5cm).

Row 1: K48, turn. Working on these 48 stitches only, continue in garter stitch stripe pattern until this section measures 5½" (14cm) from the cast-on edge. Rejoin the correct color yarn to the 48 stitches held previously and work on these stitches until this section matches the first section.

Row 2: Knit across all 96 stitches. Work 3 more rows even (2 ridges), begin decreases (keeping stripe pattern correct):

Row 3: *K10, k2tog, repeat from * to the end of the row. 88 stitches. Work 3 rows even.

Row 4: *K9, k2tog, repeat from * to the end of the row. 80 stitches. Work 3 rows even.

Row 5: *K8, k2tog, repeat from * to the end of the row. 72 stitches. Work 3 rows even.

Row 6: *K7, k2tog, repeat from * to the end of the row. 64 stitches. Work 3 rows even.

Row 7: *K6, k2tog, repeat from * to the end of the row. 56 stitches. Continue working decreases every 4th row as set until 8 stitches remain.

Row 8: *K2tog, repeat 3 times more. Cut yarn, leaving a long end and draw through the remaining 4 stitches and pull up tightly. Referring to your teapot for exact placing, sew side seam so that it fits around the teapot spout neatly.

Thread half the sequins onto the Redwood yarn and half onto the Amethyst. Using Redwood color for the Redwood stripes on the cozy, catch a stitch at the top of the first Redwood stripe with the crochet hook, make a chain to secure. *Ch5, push a sequin up the yarn close to the hook and make a chain to secure, ch5, push hook through the top of the stripe ½" (13mm) further on, make 1 chain to secure, repeat from * around the first stripe. Make another row of chain loops, this time without the sequins. Fasten off. Repeat for each stripe on the cozy. Sew in all ends.

Make a pom-pom in each color yarn, approximately 2"(5cm) in diameter and sew them to the top of the cozy.

Sparkle Tea Cozy

Work exactly as for the Pom-pom Tea Cozy, BUT holding 2 ends of the Lamé yarn together throughout. Instead of pom-poms on the top, thread 1" (2.5cm) diameter sequins onto a single end of yarn, and holding this together with the fine beading wire make a chain about 2" (5cm) long, *push a sequin up the Lamé thread and make the next chain stitch with the Lamé only to secure the sequin, chain with both the Lamé and the wire for 4" (10cm), repeat from * until all 12 sequins are on the length of wire and Lamé chain. Work a further 2"(5cm) chain, fasten off. Bend the chain into loops with a sequin at the top of each loop and sew this to the top of the cozy.

Clotted Cream Biscuits

FROM TREGOTHNAN TEA ESTATE

Makes 2 dozen biscuits

1½ cups (200 grams) all-purpose flour, plus more for rolling

¾ cup (190 grams) clotted cream

3 tablespoons (45 grams) whole milk

2 tablespoons (30ml) honey

Place flour, clotted cream, milk, and honey in a mixing bowl and mix with a wooden spoon until it forms a dough. Chill the dough for an hour in the refrigerator.

Preheat the oven to 350°F (170°C).

On a lightly floured surface, roll the dough to a thickness of about ¼ inch (6mm) and cut with a 4-inch (10cm) round pastry cutter. Place on a baking sheet and leave to rest for 10 minutes.

Bake for 6 to 8 minutes until golden. Serve warm or at room temperature.

Tregothnan Tea Estate

Tregothnan Botanic Garden
Tregothnan Estate Office
Truro TR2 4AN

Email: *garden@tregothnan.com*
www.tregothnan.com

Teas can be arranged by appointment in the historic Summer House or the Himalayan Tea House (not shown). Both are set in the stunningly beautiful 99-acre Botanic Garden.

The Estate Shop sells all the Tregothnan teas, as well as other products grown or made on the estate. At Christmastime you can buy Christmas trees grown on the estate and door wreaths and swags handwoven from the leaves and foliage grown in the Botanic Garden.

chapter four

AFTERNOON TEA

Even if you are just by yourself, there is nothing to stop you from indulging in a full English Afternoon Tea on a chilly November afternoon.

Afternoon Tea is an English institution, allegedly made popular by Anna, the seventh Duchess of Bedford, in the early 1840s. In that era, lunch was light and dinner in high society was served late, between 8:30 and 9:00 p.m. The Duchess found that she became hungry in the long stretch between lunch and dinner, and to combat this she secretly started ordering tea and cakes to be sent to her boudoir. When Anna's habit was discovered, instead of being met with scorn, it caught on as a new craze and became very fashionable to take "Afternoon Tea" between the two main meals of the day.

By the 1880s, women were changing their clothes for Afternoon Tea. Tea gowns, gloves, and hats were often worn. There was a new trade in silverware for the tea table as well as in fine china and linen.

A country tea house will have a variety of delicious foods available during Afternoon Tea.

Today Afternoon Tea is sometimes called "High Tea" but as a general rule, High Tea usually has a larger selection of cakes, tarts, biscuits, scones, and sandwiches. Originally High Tea was served slightly later and always included some kind of meat, but this does not apply today. The names for these two different tea times have become interchangeable.

It is still possible to dress up for Afternoon Tea. In London's Ritz Hotel, there is a formal dress code (jacket and tie for men, no jeans or training shoes). Tea is taken in the opulent surroundings of the Palm Court, and a pianist accompanies the proceedings. Tea at the Ritz is so popular that booking is necessary four weeks in advance.

To find a range of good locations for Afternoon Tea in the United Kingdom, check the website www.tea.co.uk. Details can be found regarding the Tea Guild's Members Directory. This organization gives awards for the best Afternoon Teas so standards will be high. For locations of tea rooms in North America, visit www.teamap.com.

Skill level: Easy.

Size: To fit a teapot approximately 19" (48.5cm) diameter.

Materials:

3 balls Rowan Pure Wool DK, 100% Wool, [1¾oz (50g), 135yd (125m)], 1 each of Enamel, Tea Rose, and Snow. (3) light
Remnants of Pure Wool DK in other colors for the stripes, including Hay, Barley, and Petal.
Size 3 (3.25mm) needles.

Gauge: 24 stitches and 32 rows to 4" (10cm) over k3, p3 rib pattern when the rib is stretched slightly.

Cast on 90 stitches using size 3 (3.25mm) needles and Enamel. Work in k3, p3 rib for 6 rows.

Row 7: *K1, m1, k2, p1, m1p, p2, repeat from * to the end of the row.

Row 8: Work now in k4, p4 ribbing, taking made stitches into the rib sections.

Row 9: Begin stripe pattern, work:

2 rows Tea Rose, 2 rows Enamel, 2 rows Tea Rose, 2 rows Barley. Split for handle:

Next row: In Enamel, pattern 60, turn. *Work on these 60 stitches only for the first half of the cozy. Work even until this section measures 2 ½" (6.5cm) from the cast-on edge, with the right side facing.

Next row: *K3, m1, k1, p3, m1p, p1, repeat from * to the end of the row. 80 stitches. Work even until this half of the cozy measures 3¾" (9.5cm). Put stitches on a holder, return to the 60 stitches held previously, and work the second half of the cozy to match the first from *, ending with the wrong side facing for the next row.

Next row: Join in Petal yarn, pattern across the 80 stitches from the second half of the Cozy, then across the 80 stitches held from the first half of the Cozy. 160 stitches.

Next row: *K1, m1, k4, p1, m1p, p4, repeat from * to the end of the row. 180 stitches. Work 2 more rows in Petal, change to Enamel and work until the Cozy measures 5½" (14cm) from the cast-on edge.

Next row: *K1, k2tog, repeat from * to the end of the row. 120 stitches. Beginning with a purl row, work 5 rows in stockinette stitch.

Next row: *With the right-hand needle, pick up the loop on the purl side of the stockinette from 5 rows below, put it onto the left-hand needle and knit it together with the 1st stitch on the needle, repeat from * to the end of the row to form a ridge. Purl 1 row.

Next row: *K10, k2tog, repeat from * to the end of the row. Change to Hay yarn and work 1 row even. 110 stitches.

Next row: *k9, k2tog, repeat from * to the end of the row. 100 stitches. Work 1 row even.

Next row: *K8, k2tog, repeat from * to the end of the row. 90 stitches. Work 1 row even. Change to Snow.

Next row: *K7, k2tog, repeat from * to the end of the row. 80 stitches. Work 1 row even. Continue with alternate decrease and even rows in Snow, working 1 stitch less between the decreases as set until you have worked the row k2tog 5 times and have 5 stitches remaining.

Finishing

Cut yarn, thread through these stitches, and draw up securely. Sew seam, leaving a gap for the spout of your teapot at the appropriate point. Make a pom-pom approximately 1½" (3.8cm) in diameter in Tea Rose and attach to the top of the Cozy.

Skill level: Intermediate.

Size: XS(S, M, L, XL, XXL).

Finished Bust: 31½(35½, 39½, 43½, 47½, 51½)" (80[90, 100, 110, 121, 131]cm).

Materials:

10(10, 11, 12, 13, 14) skeins Blue Sky Alpacas Alpaca Silk, 50% Alpaca / 50% Silk [1¾oz (50g), 146yd (133)m], 9(9, 10, 11, 12, 13) in Spring, and 1(1, 1, 1, 1, 1) in Blush. (3) light

Small amounts of other colors for the cupcakes (we used Alpaca Silk in Ruby, Peacock, Amethyst, White, and Flax.)

9 buttons, approximately ½" (13mm) in diameter.

Size 3 (3.25mm) and size 4 (3.5mm) needles.

Gauge: 24 stitches and 31½ rows to 4" (10cm) over Diamond Lattice pattern on size 4 (3.5mm) needles.

Back

Cast on 97(109, 119, 131, 145, 157) stitches using size 3 (3.25mm) needles. Work 2(2, 2, 2½, 2½, 2½)" (5[5, 5, 6, 6, 6,)cm) in k1, p1 rib. Change to size 4 (3.5mm) needles. Beginning at stitch 2(2, 3, 3, 2, 2) on the Diamond Lattice chart, work in pattern until the back measures 14¼(14½, 14½, 15, 15, 15¼)" (36[37, 37, 38, 38, 39]cm) from the cast-on edge. Decrease for armholes:

Next row: Bind off 2(3, 4, 4, 5, 5) stitches at the beginning of the next 2 rows, then 2(2, 2, 2, 4, 4) stitches at the beginning of the next 2 rows.

X-Small, Small, Medium: Bind off 1(1, 1) stitch at the beginning of the next 4(10, 10) rows. 85(89, 97) stitches. Work even until the armhole measures 8(8, 8 ¼)" (20[20, 21]cm).

Large, X-Large, XX-Large: Bind off 2(3, 3) stitches at the beginning of the next 2 rows and 1(2, 3) stitches at the beginning of the next 8(2, 2) rows. Decreases for the Large size are now finished. 107 stitches. Work even until the armhole measures 8¼" (21cm).

X-Large, XX-Large: Bind off 1(2) stitches at the beginning of the next 10(4) rows, then for size XX-Large only bind off 1 stitch at the beginning of the next 10 rows. 107(109) stitches. Work even until the armhole measures 8¼(8¾)" (21[22]cm).

Shape shoulders and back neck

Pattern 26(28, 31, 36, 36, 36) stitches, turn.

Next row: P2tog, work in pattern to the last 5(6, 6, 8, 8, 8) stitches, wt.

Next row: Work in pattern to the last 2 stitches, k2tog.

Next row: P2tog, work in pattern to the last 10(12, 12, 16, 16, 16) stitches, wt.

Next row: Work in pattern to the last 2 stitches, k2tog.

Next row: Work in pattern to the last 16(18, 19, 24, 24, 24) stitches, wt.

Next row: Work in pattern to the end of the row.

Next row: Pattern all stitches, working wraps with wrapped stitches. Bind off. Bind off the central 26(28, 31, 36, 36, 36) stitches, work in pattern to the end of the row.

Next row: Work in pattern to the last 2 stitches, p2tog.

Next row: K2tog, work in pattern to the last 5(6, 6, 8, 8, 8) stitches, wt.

Next row: Work in pattern to the last 2 stitches, wt.

Next row: K2tog, work in pattern to the last 10(12, 12, 16, 16, 16) stitches, wt.

Next row: Work in pattern to the end of the row.

Next row: Pattern all stitches, working wraps with wrapped stitches. Bind off.

Left front

Cast on 53(59, 64, 70, 77, 83) stitches using size 3 (3.25mm) needles. Work 2(2, 2, 2½, 2½, 2½)" (5[5, 5, 6, 6, 6]cm) in k1, p1 rib. Change to size 4 (3.5mm) needles. Beginning at stitch 6(6, 4, 4, 2, 2) on the Diamond Lattice chart, work in pattern for 48(54, 59, 65, 72, 78) stitches. Place the remaining 5 stitches onto a holder for the button band. Work even until the front measures 14¼(14½, 14½, 15, 15, 15¼)" (36[37, 37, 38, 38, 39]cm) from the cast-on edge, ending with the right side of the front facing for the next row. Decrease for armholes, but note:

When the armhole measures approximately 1¼(1¼, 1¾, 1¾, 1¾, 1¾)" (3[3, 4.5, 4.5, 4.5, 4.5]cm), you will need to start the Cupcake chart on the next 2nd row of the Diamond Lattice chart (a wrong-side row). At this point, while keeping the armhole decreases correct, pattern 9(9, 15, 15, 15, 15), work across the 30 stitches of the Cupcake chart, work in pattern to the end of the row.

Next row: Bind off 2(3, 4, 4, 5, 5) stitches at the beginning of the next row, work 1 row even, bind off 2(2, 2, 2, 4, 4) stitches at the beginning of the next row.

X-Small, Small, Medium: Bind off 1(1, 1) stitch at the beginning of the next 2(5, 5) right-side rows. 42(44, 48) stitches.

Large, X-Large, XX-Large: Bind off 2(3, 3) stitches at the beginning of the next row and 1(2, 3) stitches at the beginning of the next 4(1, 1) right-side rows. Decreases for the Large size are now finished. 53 stitches.

X-Large, XX-Large: Bind off 1(2) stitches at the beginning of the next 5(2) right-side rows, then for size XX-Large only bind off 1 stitch at the beginning of the next 5 right-side rows. 53(54) stitches.

Work now from the chart for the Cupcake intarsia design, starting the front neck shaping when the front measures 18¼(18½, 18¾, 19¼, 19¼, 20)" (46[47, 47.5, 49, 49, 51]cm) from the cast-on edge, and with the wrong side of the front facing you.

Bind off 4 stitches at the beginning of the next 2 wrong-side rows, then 2 stitches at the beginning of the following wrong-side row. Bind off 2 stitches at the beginning of the next 1(1, 1, 1, 2, 2) wrong-side rows, then 1 stitch at the beginning of the following 7(7, 8, 8, 7, 7) rows. Work even until the armhole matches the back armhole to the shoulder shaping, with the wrong side of the work facing. 8(8, 8¼, 8¼, 8¾)" (20[20, 21, 21, 22]cm). Shape shoulder:

Next row: Work in pattern to the last 5(6, 6, 8, 8, 8) stitches, wt.

Next row: Work in pattern to the end of the row.

Next row: Work in pattern to the last 10(12, 12, 16, 16, 16) stitches, wt.

Next row: Work in pattern to the end of the row.

Next row: Work in pattern to the last 16(18, 19, 24, 24, 24) stitches, wt.

Next row: Work in pattern to the end of the row.

Next row (wrong side): Bind off, working wraps with wrapped stitches.

Right front

Cast on 53(59, 64, 70, 77, 83) stitches using size 3 (3.25mm) needles. Work 4 rows in k1, p1 rib.

Next row: Rib 2, bind off 2 stitches for the buttonhole, rib to end.

Next row: Rib, casting on 2 stitches over those bound off. Work even until the ribbing measures 2(2, 2, 2½, 2½, 2½)" (5[5, 5, 6, 6, 6]cm) in k1, p1 rib. Rib 5, place these stitches on a holder for the buttonhole band, change to size 4 (3.5mm)

needles. Beginning at stitch 6 on the chart, work in Diamond Lattice pattern for 48(54, 59, 65, 72, 78) stitches. Work even until the front measures 14¼(14½, 14½, 15, 15, 15¼)" (36[37, 37, 38, 38, 39]cm) from the cast-on edge, ending with the wrong side of the front facing for the next row. Decrease for armholes:

Next row: Bind off 2(3, 4, 4, 5, 5) stitches at the beginning of the next row, work 1 row even, bind off 2(2, 2, 2, 4, 4) stitches at the beginning of the next row.

X-Small, Small, Medium: Bind off 1(1, 1) stitch at the beginning of the next 2(5, 5) wrong-side rows. 42(44, 48) stitches.

Large, X-Large, XX-Large: Bind off 2(3, 3) stitches at the beginning of the next row and 1(2, 3) stitches at the beginning of the next 4(1, 1) wrong-side rows. Decreases for the Large size are now finished. 53 stitches.

X-Large, XX-Large: Bind off 1(2) stitches at the beginning of the next 5(2) wrong-side rows, then for size XX-Large only bind off 1 stitch at the beginning of the next 5 wrong-side rows. 53(54) stitches.

Work even until the front measures 18¼(18½, 18¾, 19¼, 19¼, 20)" (46[47, 47.5, 49, 49, 51]cm) from the cast-on edge, and with the right side of the front facing you.

Bind off 4 stitches at the beginning of the next 2 right-side rows, then 2 stitches at the beginning of the following right-side row. Bind off 2 stitches at the beginning of the next 1(1, 1, 1, 2, 2) right-side rows, then 1 stitch at the beginning of the following 7(7, 8, 8, 7, 7) right-side rows. Work even until the armhole matches the back armhole to the shoulder shaping, with the right side of the work facing. 8(8, 8¼, 8¼, 8¼, 8¾)" (20[20, 21, 21, 22]cm).

Shape shoulder

Next row: Work in pattern to the last 5(6, 6, 8, 8, 8) stitches, wt.

Next row: Work in pattern to the end of the row.

Next row: Work in pattern to the last 10(12, 12, 16, 16, 16) stitches, wt.

Next row: Work in pattern to the end of the row.

Next row: Work in pattern to the last 16(18, 19, 24, 24, 24) stitches, wt.

Next row: Work in pattern to the end of the row.

Next row: Bind off, working wraps with wrapped stitches.

Sleeves

Cast on 41(41, 45, 45, 49, 49) stitches using size 3 (3.25mm) needles. Work 2(2, 2, 2½, 2½, 2½)" (5[5, 5, 6, 6, 6]cm) in k1, p1 rib. Change to size 4 (3.5mm) needles. Starting at stitch 6(6, 4, 4, 2, 2), work in Diamond Lattice pattern for 4 rows.

Next row: K1, m1, work in pattern to last stitch, m1, k1.

Continue now increasing on every following 4th row 15(19, 19, 19, 19, 18) times, and then every following 6th row 7(5, 5, 5, 5, 6) times. 87(91, 95, 95, 99, 99) stitches. Work even until the sleeve measures 15¾" (40cm) from the cast-on edge.

Cupcake Cardigan chart

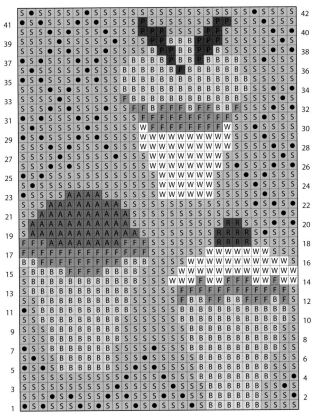

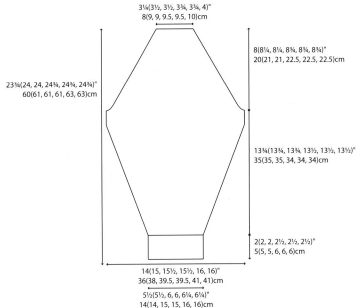

3¼(3½, 3½, 3¾, 3¾, 4)"
8(9, 9, 9.5, 9.5, 10)cm

8(8¼, 8¼, 8¾, 8¾, 8¾)"
20(21, 21, 22.5, 22.5, 22.5)cm

23¾(24, 24, 24¾, 24¾, 24¾)"
60(61, 61, 61, 63, 63)cm

13¾(13¾, 13¾, 13½, 13½, 13½)"
35(35, 35, 34, 34, 34)cm

2(2, 2, 2½, 2½, 2½)"
5(5, 5, 6, 6, 6)cm

14(15, 15½, 15½, 16, 16)"
36(38, 39.5, 39.5, 41, 41)cm

5½(5½, 6, 6, 6¼, 6¼)"
14(14, 15, 15, 16, 16)cm

14(14½, 16, 17½, 17½, 18)"
35.5(37, 40.5, 44.5, 44.5, 45.5)cm

5(5¼, 5¾, 6½, 6½, 6½)"
12.5(13, 14.5, 16.5, 16.5, 16.5)cm

5"(12.5cm)

1" (2.5cm)

8(8, 8¼, 8¼, 8¼, 8¾)"
20(20, 21, 21, 21, 22)cm

14½(14½, 14½, 15, 15, 15¼)"
36(37, 37, 38, 38, 39)cm

23½(23½, 23¾, 24¼, 24¼, 25)"
58.5(59.5, 60.5, 61.5, 61.5, 63.5)cm

2(2, 2, 2½, 2½, 2½)"
5(5, 5, 6, 6, 6)cm

15¾(17¾, 19¾, 21¾, 23¾, 25¾)"
40(45, 50, 55, 60.5, 65.5)cm

S	'Spring' stitch	A	'Amethyst' stitch
●	'Spring' stitch. Purl on the right side, knit on the wrong side.	B	'Blush' stitch
		F	'Flax' stitch
R	'Ruby' stitch	P	'Peacock' stitch

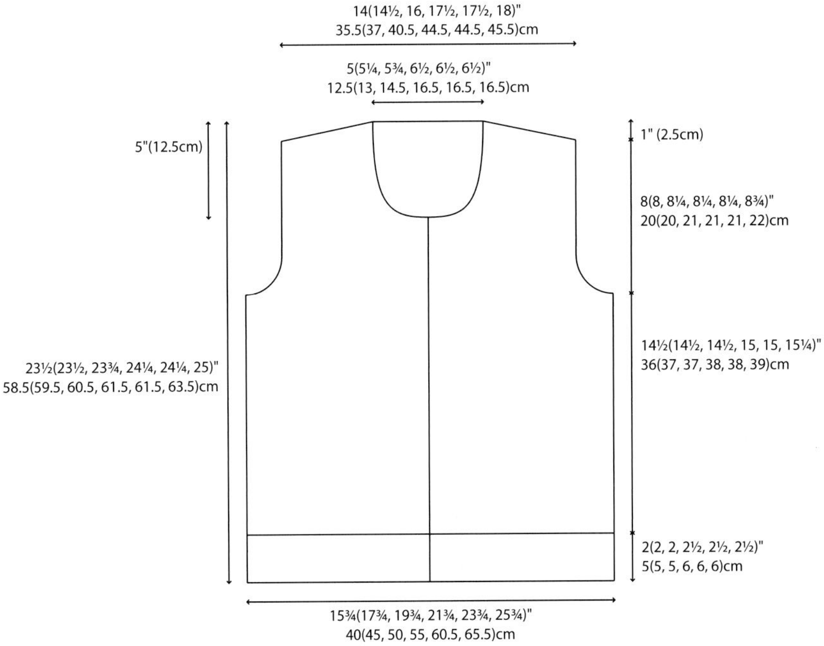

Diamond Lattice chart for Cupcake Cardigan

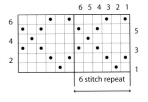

6 5 4 3 2 1

6 stitch repeat

Shape sleeve cap

Bind off 3 stitches at the beginning of the next 2 rows, 2 stitches at the beginning of the following 2 rows 1(1, 1, 2, 2, 3) times, and then 1 stitch at the beginning of the next 10 rows.

Work 2 rows even. Bind off 1 stitch at the beginning of the next 2 rows. Repeat from * once, then bind off 1 stitch at the beginning of every row until 19(21, 21, 23, 23, 25) stitches remain. Bind off.

Sew the shoulder seams.

Button band

With the right side of the Left Front facing, slip the stitches held for the button band to a size 3 (3.25mm) needle. Rejoin yarn, kfb, rib to the end of the row. 6 stitches. Work in k1, p1 rib until band reaches to the beginning of the neck shaping when slightly stretched. Slip stitch into place. Mark on 8 button positions, one to correspond with the buttonhole already worked in the Right Front, and the other 7 spread evenly up the front. The final buttonhole will be worked in the neckband.

Buttonhole band

With the wrong side of the right front facing, slip the stitches held for the buttonhole band onto a size 3 (3.25mm) needle. Rejoin yarn, kfb, rib to the end of the row. Work in k1, p1 rib as for button band, working buttonholes to correspond with button positions marked on the button band. When the band reaches the front neck shaping, rib 4, k2tog, pick up and knit 34(34, 34, 36, 36, 36) stitches up the right front neck, 48(48, 49, 49, 50, 52) stitches around the back neck, 34(34, 34, 36, 36, 36) down the left front neck, k2tog from the button band, rib 4. Work 1 row in k1, p1 rib. Work buttonhole in the next row:

Next row: Rib 2, bind off 2 stitches, rib to the end of the row. Work 4 more rows in rib, bind off.

Finishing

Embroider cupcakes with Ruby and Silver French knots. Sew in all ends. Set in sleeves, sew side and sleeve seams. Sew on buttons.

STRIPED GLOVES

Skill level: Intermediate.

Size: to fit average hand, approximately 7½–8" (19–20.5cm) circumference.

Materials:

3 skeins Blue Sky Alpacas Alpaca Silk, 50% Alpaca / 50% Silk [1¾oz (50g), 146yd (133)m], 1 each of Amethyst, Plum, and Spring. (3) light
You should be able to make 2 pairs of gloves out of 3 skeins of yarn.
Size 4 (3.5mm) needles.

Gauge: 24 stitches and 30 rows to 4" (10cm) over stockinette stitch on size 3 needles.

The gloves are worked flat, using the intarsia technique, and then sewn together from the top of each finger to the hand
and from the top of the thumb to the wrist.

Cut lengths of yarn to use for each stripe. Each glove needs 8 Plum, 4 Spring, and 4 Amethyst.
3yds (3m) is long enough that you won't have lots and lots of ends to darn in, but the lengths won't get too tangled as you work.

Both Gloves

Cast on 48 stitches using size 4 (3.5mm) needles and Plum. The long-tail or Continental method is better than the cable cast-on for this. Set up the intarsia stripes.

Right Glove

Next row: *K3 Plum, k3 Spring, k3 Plum, k3 Amethyst, repeat from * to the end of the row.

Next row (and all wrong-side rows): Purl stitches, twisting yarns together to avoid holes forming.

Work 2" (5cm) in stockinette intarsia, ending with the right side of the glove facing for the next row. Change to k2, p2 ribbing, keeping the intarsia stripes correct and work 1" (2.5cm), again ending with the right side of the glove facing. Work a further ½" (13mm) (or the length you require to reach to the base of your thumb) in stockinette intarsia.

Begin thumb gusset

Next row: K1, m1, work in pattern to the last stitch, m1, k1. Take the increased stitches into the edge stripe colors.

Next row: Purl in intarsia. Repeat these 2 rows 9 times more, you will have 13 stitches in each edge section. 68 stitches.

Next row: Work in pattern to the last 10 stitches, turn. Leave these stitches on a holder for one half of the thumb. Repeat this row once more, you will have 20 stitches held for the thumb and 48 stitches to work on for the hand. Work even on these stitches in pattern for 1½" (3.8cm) or until the glove reaches to the base of your fingers.

Little finger

With the right side of the glove facing, slip the first 19 stitches of the hand onto a holder. (This is the "1st holder" in the following instructions.) Rejoin yarn to the next stitch in the appropriate color:

Next row: Kfb, k8, kfb in pattern. 12 stitches. Put the remaining 19 stitches onto another holder (the "2nd holder"). Work on these 12 stitches until the finger reaches just to the top of your little finger, with the right side of the work facing.

Next row: K2tog 6 times. 6 stitches. Thread yarn through these 6 stitches twice and draw up tightly. Leave a long tail to help with sewing up.

Ring finger

With the right side of the glove facing, slip the first 5 stitches from the 2nd holder onto the left-hand needle, then slip the last 5 stitches from the 1st holder onto the same needle (these are the 2 sets of stitches nearest to the little finger just worked). Join the appropriate colored yarn to the first stitch, then:

Next row: Kfb, pattern 3, kfb twice, pattern 3, kfb. 14 stitches. With the wrong side of the glove facing you, you will have 2 Amethyst stitches, 3 Plum, 2 Spring, 2 Plum, 3 Spring, 2 Plum. Work on these 14 stitches until the finger reaches just to the top of your ring finger, with the right side of the glove facing.

Next row: K2tog 7 times. 7 stitches. Thread yarn through these 6 stitches twice and draw up tightly. Leave a long tail to help with sewing up.

Middle finger

With the right side of the glove facing, slip the first 6 stitches from the 2nd holder onto the left-hand needle, then slip the last 6 stitches from the 1st holder onto the same needle. Join the appropriate colored yarn to the first stitch, then:

Next row: Kfb, pattern 4, kfb twice, pattern 4, kfb. 16 stitches. With the wrong side of the glove facing you, you will have 2 Spring stitches, 3 Plum, 3 Amethyst, 3 Plum, 3 Amethyst, 2 Plum. Work on these 16 stitches until the finger reaches just to the top of your middle finger, with the right side of the glove facing.

Next row: K2tog 8 times. 8 stitches. Thread yarn through these 6 stitches twice and draw up tightly. Leave a long tail to help with sewing up.

Index finger

With the right side of the glove facing, slip the remaining stitches from each holder back to the left-hand needle. Rejoin the appropriate colored yarn to the first stitch:

Next row: Kfb, k6, kfb twice, k6, kfb. 20 stitches. With the wrong side of the glove facing you, you will have 4 Amethyst stitches, 3 Plum, 3 Spring, 3 Plum, 3 Spring, 4 Amethyst. Work on these 20 stitches until the finger reaches just to the top of your index finger, with the right side of the glove facing.

Next row: K2tog 10 times.

Next row: P2tog 5 times. 5 stitches. Thread yarn through these 5 stitches twice and draw up tightly. Leave a long tail of yarn to help with sewing up.

Thumb

With the right side of the glove facing, slip the 10 stitches from each holder for the thumb back onto the left-hand needle, rejoin the appropriate colored yarn to the first stitch and work across these 20 stitches. With the wrong side of the glove facing you, you will have 10 Amethyst and 10 Plum stitches. Work on these stitches until the thumb reaches just to the top of your thumb, with the right side of the glove facing.

Next row: K2tog 10 times.

Next row: P2tog 5 times. 5 stitches. Thread yarn through these 5 stitches twice and draw up tightly. Leave a long tail of yarn to help with sewing up.

Left Glove

Set up the intarsia stripes:

Next row: *K3 Amethyst, k3 Plum, k3 Spring, k3 Plum, repeat from * to the end of the row.

Next row (and all wrong-side rows): Purl stitches, twisting yarns together to avoid holes forming.

Work left glove as for the right glove, noting that the sequence of colors when working the fingers will be reversed.

Finishing

Sew in all ends, sew the open edge of each finger with the long tail of yarn left for this purpose using mattress stitch, and only taking in half of each edge stitch for the neatest fit.

Skill level: Easy / Intermediate.

Size: to fit average head, approximately 21–22" (53.5–56cm) circumference.

Materials:

6 skeins Blue Sky Alpacas Alpaca Silk, 50% Alpaca / 50% Silk [1¾oz (50g), 146yd (133)m], 1 each of Peacock, Sapphire, Blush, Amethyst, Plum, and Spring. (3) light

The beret in a single color would take 1 skein only, so if you make the striped version, you should be able to make 2 pairs of Striped Gloves to match.

Size 3 (3.25mm) double-pointed needles or circular needle if you prefer to use the magic loop technique.

Gauge: 22 stitches and 30 rows to 4" (10cm) over stockinette stitch on size 3 needles.

Stripe sequence: 4 rounds each of Peacock, Sapphire, Blush, Plum, Amethyst, and Spring, repeated until the beret is finished.

Cast on 110 stitches using size 3 (3.25mm) needles and Peacock. Join into a round being careful not to twist the stitches and either arrange evenly over the double-pointed needles or for the magic loop technique. Work 4 rounds of twisted rib: *K1tbl, p1, repeat from * around. Change to Sapphire and work 2 rounds twisted rib.

Next round: *M1, k5, repeat from * around. 132 stitches. Work 3 rounds even (changing color to Blush after the 4 rounds of Sapphire).

Next round: *M1, k6 around. 154 stitches. Work 3 rounds even (changing color to Plum after 4 rounds of Blush).

Next round: *M1, k7 around. 176 stitches. Work 3 rounds even, again changing color at the appropriate time.

Now begin decreases for crown of beret

Next round: *K20, k2tog, repeat from * around. 168 stitches. Work 1 round even.

Next round: k10, k2tog, *k19, k2tog, repeat from * to the last 9 stitches, k9. 160 stitches. Work 1 round even.

Next round: *K18. k2tog, repeat from * around. 152 stitches. Work 1 round even.

Next round: K9, k2tog, *k17, k2tog, repeat from * to the last 8 stitches, k8. 144 stitches. Work 1 round even.

Continue with decreases as set, decreasing 8 stitches every other round until there are 16 stitches remaining.

Next round: K2tog 8 times. 8 stitches.

Finishing

Cut yarn, thread through these 8 stitches, draw up and fasten off securely. Sew in ends.

Skill level: Intermediate.

Size: Finished cushion cover is approximately 20" (51cm) in diameter.

Materials:

9 balls Rowan Pure Wool Aran, 100% wool [3½ oz (100g), 184yd (170m)], 4 balls in Ivory and 1 ball each of Noir, Charcoal, and Pepper. (4) medium

Size 6 (4mm) needles.

Gauge: 18 stitches and 36 rows to 4" (10cm) over garter stitch on size 6 (4mm) needles.

Front

Cast on 48 stitches using size 6 (4mm) needles and Noir. Work in garter stitch (every row knit) throughout.

*Work 2 rows garter stitch (1 ridge facing on the right side).

K40, turn, and knit back.

K32, turn, and knit back.

K24, turn, and knit back.

K16, turn, and knit back.

K8, turn, and knit back. This completes 1 segment**.

Repeat from * once more in Noir.

Repeat from * twice in Charcoal.

Repeat from * twice in Pepper.

Repeat from * twice in Ivory.

Repeat this whole 4-color sequence 5 times more. Bind off, cut yarn, leaving a long tail, and thread this through the inner edge of the segments. Draw up tightly to close. Sew bound-off edge to cast-on edge.

Edge

Cast on 14 stitches using size 6 (4mm) needles and Ivory. Work in garter stitch, slipping the first stitch of each row until the strip fits all around the front. Bind off, sew bound-off edge to cast-on edge, and sew neatly to front.

Back (2 pieces)

Cast on 48 stitches using size 6 (4mm) needles and Ivory. Work in segment pattern from * to ** in Ivory only until you have worked 25 segments. Do not bind off, knit across the 48 stitches on needles, pick up and knit 48 stitches from the cast-on edge of the piece. 96 stitches. Work back and forth in rows over entire width, decreasing 1 stitch at each end of every 3rd row until this border is 2¼" (5.5cm) deep. Bind off. Thread yarn through the inner edge of segments and draw up tightly to close. Make another piece the same.

Finishing

Sew both back pieces to the edge of the cushion with each full-width garter stitch band overlapping the other, creating an envelope back for the cushion.

Using all 4 colors of yarn, make a large tassel and stitch in the middle of the front.

Bakewell Tart

FROM CHARLOTTE'S TEA HOUSE

Makes one 9-inch (23cm) tart; serves 10

TART DOUGH

1 stick (113 grams) unsalted butter, chilled

2 cups (280 grams) all-purpose flour, plus more for rolling

Up to 4 tablespoons (60 ml) ice water

FILLING

1 stick (113 grams) unsalted butter

½ cup (100 grams) confectioner's sugar

3 heaping tablespoons (80 grams)
self-raising flour

¾ cup (75 grams) ground almonds

1 teaspoon (5ml) almond extract

1 teaspoon (3g) baking powder

2 large eggs

2 tablespoons (30ml) whole milk

1 cup (350g) raspberry jam

To make the tart dough, cut the butter into the flour until the texture of the mixture resembles coarse crumbs.

Stir in just enough water to form into a dough. Gather into a ball, pat into a disk, and cover with plastic wrap. Refrigerate for 1 hour. On a lightly floured surface, roll the dough until it is ¼ -inch (6mm) thick. Fit the dough into a 9-inch (23cm) tart pan. Refrigerate for 30 minutes. Dough must be pre-baked for 15 minutes, with a layer of aluminum foil on top and dried peas or rice scattered on top of that (to stop the pastry from rising), then another 5–10 minutes with the foil removed, before filling goes in.

Preheat the oven to 375°F (191°C).

To make the filling, in an electric mixer, beat together the butter, confectioner's sugar, flour, ground almonds, almond extract, baking powder, eggs, and milk.

Spread the raspberry jam over the bottom of the tart shell and then pour the filling mixture on top. Bake for 40 minutes on or until a metal skewer inserted in the center comes out dry.

Cool on a wire rack before unmolding.

ICING

After the tart has cooled, measure out 12 tablespoons (320g) of confectioner's sugar into a bowl, gradually adding one tablespoon of warm water at a time to the sugar until the mixture is a thick but pourable consistency.

Using the back of a tablespoon dipped in hot water, spread mixture onto the tart until you have covered top of the tart.

Decorate with candied cherries if desired.

Charlotte's Tea House

The Coinage Hall
One Boscawen Street
Truro
TR1 2QU
United Kingdom

teahouse@tiscali.co.uk

Charlotte's Tea House is a traditional country tea house serving a wide variety of teas and homemade cakes, desserts, tarts, and sandwiches. The tea house, described as "a sanctuary of Victorian tranquility," is on the first floor of the Coinage Hall, which was built in 1848 and overlooks the busy center of Truro.

chapter five

BUILDER'S TEA

The term *Builders' Tea* is a relatively new addition to the English language and one that could puzzle anyone born outside the United Kingdom. It refers to the strong pungent tea consumed in great quantities by English builders (construction workers) as well as truck drivers—most of whom are men. This tea is usually drunk with milk and often with vast amounts of sugar.

Builder's Tea is not a particular type of tea, more a strength of tea. It is always served at "transport cafés" found at the sides of all the major motorways (highways) in the United Kingdom. This style of tea is brewed up on construction sites large and small, all over the country. Builders have even been known to refuse to work unless a kettle, mugs, and tea bags are provided by their employers. No self-respecting builders would go without their "tea breaks." These "down tools" (breaks) can last anywhere from fifteen to thirty minutes and can occur at varying times during the working day.

A transport café (truck stop) is the perfect (although unlikey-looking) place to have a cup of Builder's Tea.

Truck drivers also take tea breaks, which allow them to be able to have a rest and sit down with a nice "cuppa" (mug of strong tea) to punctuate their long journey.

You know you are in an authentic transport café (pronounced "caff" by their customers) if you are served tea from a large tea urn into a mug rather than a cup and saucer.

Builder's Tea is usually sold as tea bags and is cheap and strong. There is a saying that the tea should be so strong that you can "stand a spoon up in it." This phrase may also refer to the quantity of sugar in the tea.

As with most teas, Builder's Tea can be consumed at any time of day and is excellent with the vast English breakfast known as a "fry up." This is a combination of fried eggs, bacon, sausages, black pudding, tomatoes, mushrooms, baked beans, and a fried slice of bread that soaks up all the cholesterol-loaded juices!

Later on in the day, Builder's Tea goes down well with a large slab of homemade cake or a delicious dessert. A mug of this tea is, for many, the perfect complement to another English traditional meal, fish and chips.

Builder's Tea has become so much a part of the language that today, when you are asked how you would like your tea, if you reply "Builder's," your hostess or waitress will know immediately that you like your tea really strong!

Builder's Tea is the opposite of fine teas, such as orange pekoe or rose pouchong, which have delicate and sophisticated flavors, and which are usually served in refined tea rooms or tea gardens.

Tea drinking is a custom that spreads across all social boundaries and working hierarchies—from the factory floor to the boardroom.

Left: Inside a transport café.

Above: Settling down for a huge slice of Coffee and Walnut Cake (see page 120) and a "fry up."

Skill level: Intermediate.

Size: S(M, L, XL).

Finished Chest: 41½(45½, 49½, 53½)" (105.5[115.5, 125.5, 136]cm).

Materials:

19(20, 22, 23) balls Karabella Aurora 8, 100% Merino Wool l [1¾oz (50g), 98yd(90m)], Steel. (4) medium

Gauge: 25½ stitches and 26 rows to 4" (10cm) over cable pattern on size 7 (4.5mm) needles.

Size 6 (4mm) and size 7 (4.5mm) needles.

Back

Cast on 118(122, 130, 142) stitches using size 6 (4mm) needles. Work 21 rows k2, p2 rib. Next row:

Small: *Pattern 6, m1p, (pattern 5, m1p) 10 times, repeat from * once, end pattern 6. 140 stitches.

Medium: *Pattern 5, m1p, pattern 4, m1p, repeat from * to the last 5 stitches, m1p, pattern 5. 148 stitches.

Large: Pattern 5, m1p, (pattern 4, m1p) 5 times, *pattern 5, m1p, (pattern 4, m1p) 8 times, repeat from * once, pattern 5, m1p, (pattern 4, m1p) 5 times, end pattern 5. 160 stitches.

X-Large: Pattern 6, m1p, *pattern 4 m1p, pattern 5, m1p, repeat from * to the last 10 stitches, end pattern 4, m1p, pattern 6. 172 stitches.

Change to size 7 (4.5mm) needles and begin pattern:

Small:

Row 1: (K1, p1) 5 times, work row 1 of chart C, p1, C, B, C, A, C, B, C, A, C, B, C, p1, C, (p1, k1) 5 times.

Row 2: (K1, p1) 5 times, work row 2 of charts, end (p1, k1) 5 times. The 10 stitches of seed stitch repeat at each side of the work.

Medium:

Row 1: (K1, p1) 3 times, k1, work row 1 of chart A, C, B, C, A, C, B, C, A, C, B, C, A, (k1, p1) 3 times, k1.

Row 2: (K1, p1) 3 times, k1, work row 2 of charts, end (k1, p1) 3 times, k1. 7 stitches of seed stitch repeat at each side of work.

Large, X-Large:

Row 1: (K1, p1) 5(8) times, work row 1 of chart C, A, C, B, C, A, C, B, C, A, C, B, C, A, C, (p1, k1) 5(8) times.

Row 2: (K1, p1) 5(8) times, k1, work row 2 of charts, end (p1, k1) 5(8) times. 10(16) stitches of seed stitch repeat at each side of work.

Work even in pattern as set until the back measures 16(16¼, 16½, 17)" (40.5[41.5, 42, 43]cm), from the cast-on edge with the right side of the work facing for the next row. Bind off 3 stitches at the beginning of the next 2 rows, then 1 stitch at the beginning of the next 8 rows. 126(134, 146, 158) stitches**.

Work even until armhole measures 10¼(10½, 11, 11)" (26[26.5, 28, 28]cm). Shape shoulder and back neck:

Next row: Pattern 31(35, 39, 45), turn.

Next row: P2tog, work in pattern to the end of the row.

Next row (right side): Bind off 10(11, 12, 14) stitches, work in pattern to the last 2 stitches, k2tog.

Next row: P2tog, work in pattern to the end.

Next row: Bind off 9(11, 12, 14) stitches, work in pattern to the end.

Next row: Work in pattern to the end.

Next row: Bind off the remaining 9(10, 12, 14) stitches.

Slip the center 64(64, 68, 68) stitches to a holder for the back neck, rejoin yarn to the remaining 31(35, 39, 45) stitches, work in pattern to the end of the row.

Next row (wrong side): Bind off 10(11, 12, 14) stitches, work in pattern to the last 2 stitches, p2tog.

Next row: K2tog, work in pattern to the end.

Next row: Bind off 9(11, 12, 14) stitches, work in pattern to the last 2 stitches, p2tog.

Next row: Work in pattern to the end.

Next row: Bind off the remaining 9(10, 12, 14) stitches.

Front

Work as for the back to **. Work straight until armhole measures 7(7¼, 7½, 7½)" (18[18.5, 19, 19]cm). Shape front neck:

Next row: Pattern 53(57, 63, 69), turn.

Bind off 4 stitches at the beginning of this next row, and then 3 stitches 3 times, 2 stitches 4(4, 5, 5) times, and 1 stitch 4 times on the following wrong-side rows. 28(32, 36, 42) stitches. Work even until the armhole measures 10¼(10½, 11, 11)" (26[26.5, 28, 28]cm), bind off 10(11, 12, 14) stitches at the beginning of the next row, then 9(11, 12, 14) stitches at the beginning of the next right-side row and the remaining 9(10, 12, 14) stitches on the next right-side row. Slip the central 20 stitches to a holder for the front neck, rejoin yarn to the remaining stitches, and work in pattern to the end of the row. Work 1 row even.

Next row: Bind off 4 stitches at the beginning of this next row, and then 3 stitches 3 times, 2 stitches 4(4, 5, 5) times, and 1 stitch 4 times on the following right-side rows. 28(32, 36, 42) stitches. Work even until the armhole measures 10¼(10½, 11, 11)" (26[26.5, 28, 28]cm), with the wrong side of the front facing, bind off 10(11, 12, 14) stitches at the beginning of the next row, then 9(11, 12, 14) stitches at the

beginning of the next wrong-side row and the remaining 9(10, 12, 14) stitches on the next wrong-side row.

Sleeves

Cast on 48(48, 52, 52) stitches with size 6 (4mm) needles. Work 21 rows k2, p2 rib.

Small, Medium:

Next row: Rib 3, m1p, *pattern 2, m1p, repeat from * to the last 3 stitches, rib 3. 70 stitches.

Large, X-Large:

Next row: *Rib 2, m1p, rib3, m1p, repeat from * to the last 2 stitches, rib 2. 72 stitches.

Change to size 7 (4.5mm) needles and work cable pattern as follows:

Row 1: (k1, p1) 2(2, 3, 3) times, k1 1(1, 0, 0) times, work row 1 of chart C, A, C, B, C, A C, (k1, p1) 2(2, 3, 3) times, k1 1(1, 0, 0) times.

Row 2: (k1, p1) 2(2, 3, 3) times, k1 1(1, 0, 0) times, work row 2 of charts, (k1, p1) 2(2, 3, 3) times, k1 1(1, 0, 0) times.

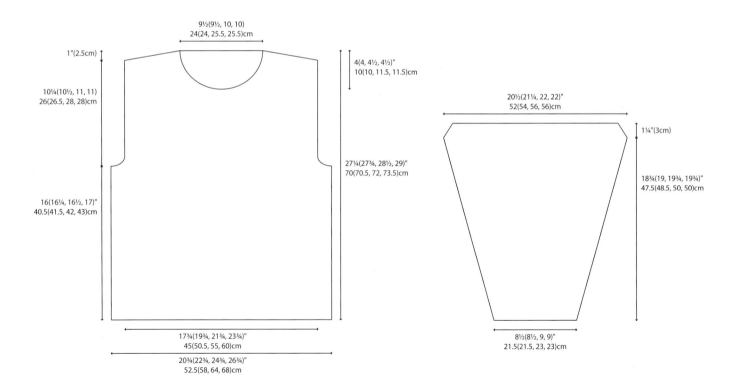

Increase at each end of the 5th pattern row, then *every following 4th, every following 6th row (2 increases in every 10 rows) until there are 110(114, 118, 118) stitches, taking increased stitches into seed stitch panels at the sides of the sleeves. Work even until the sleeve measures 18¾(19, 19¾, 19¾)" (47.5[48.5, 50, 50]cm). Bind off 3 stitches at the beginning of the next 2 rows, then 1 stitch at each end of the next 4 right-side rows. Bind off.

Neckband

Join the right shoulder seam. With size 6 (4mm) needles and the right side of the work facing, pick up and knit 22(22, 24, 24) stitches down the left side of the front neck, 20 stitches from the holder across the front neck, 22(22, 24, 24) stitches up the left side of the front neck, 2 stitches down the right back neck, 64(64, 68, 68) stitches from the holder for the back neck, and 2 stitches up the left back neck. 132(132, 136, 136) stitches. Work 4" (10cm) in k2, p2 rib, bind off in rib.

Sew left shoulder and neckband seam. Set in sleeves, sew side and sleeve seams. Sew in all ends.

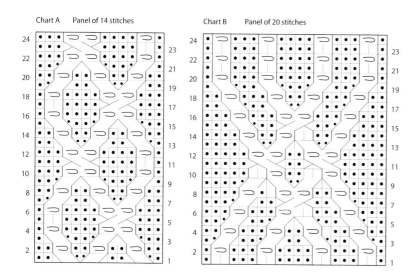

Chart A   Panel of 14 stitches

Chart B   Panel of 20 stitches

Chart C

Panel of 3 stitches

•	Purl on the right side, knit on the wrong side.
⊘	Knit through the back of the loop (k1tbl).
⌐	Bind these 2 stitches. Yarn over, p2, pass the yo over the 2 purled stitches.
⟍	Slip 2 stitches onto a cable needle and hold at the front of the work, p1, k2 from the cable needle.
⟋	Slip 1 stitch onto a cable needle and hold at the back of the work, k2, p1 from the cable needle.
⟍	Slip 2 stitches onto a cable needle and hold at the back of the work, k2, k2 from the cable needle.
⟋	Slip 2 stitches onto a cable needle and hold at the front of the work, k2, k2 from the cable needle.
⟋	Slip 2 stitches onto a cable needle and hold at the front of the work, k1tbl from the left-hand needle, slip the purl stitch from the cable needle back to the left-hand needle and purl it, then knit the remaining stitch on the cable needle tbl.

Skill level: Easy.

Size: XS(S, M, L, XL, XXL).

Finished Bust: 32(36, 40, 44, 48, 52)" (81[91, 101.5, 112, 122, 132]cm).

Materials:

14(15, 16, 17, 18, 19) balls Karabella Aurora Bulky, 100% Merino Wool [1¾oz (50g), 54yd (50m)], Palest Pink. (5) bulky
Size 9 (5.5mm) and size 10½ (6.5mm) needles.

Gauge: 13½ stitches and 21 rows to 4" (10cm) over stockinette stitch on size 10½ needles.

7 buttons, approximately 1" (2.5cm) diameter.

Back

Cast on 47(55, 61, 67, 75, 81) stitches using size 9 (5.5mm) needles. Work 6 rows (3 ridges) in garter stitch. Change to size 10½ (6.5mm) needles and continue in stockinette stitch, increasing 1 stitch at each end of the 9th and every following 10th row until there are 55(63, 69, 75, 83, 89) stitches. (Increase row: K2, m1, k to last 2 stitches, m1, k2.)

Work even until the back measures 10½(10½, 10¾, 11, 11, 11½)" (26.5[26.5, 27, 28, 28, 29]cm) from the cast-on edge, with the right side of the work facing for the next row.

Shape armholes

X-Small: Bind off 2 stitches at the beginning of the next 2 rows, then 1 stitch at the beginning of the next 4 rows. 47 stitches.

Small, Medium, Large, X-Large, XX-Large: Bind off 3(3, 3, 3, 4) stitches at the beginning of the next 2 rows, 2(2, 2, 2, 3) stitches on the following 2 rows, and 1(1, 1, 1, 0) stitches on the 6(10, 10, 0, 0) following rows. **X-Large and XX-Large:** 2(2) stitches at the beginning of the next 2(4) rows, followed by 1 stitch at each end of the next 6(4) rows. 47(49, 55, 57, 59) stitches.

Work even until the back measures 14¼(14¼, 14½, 15, 15, 15½)" (36[36, 37, 38, 38, 39.5]cm) from the cast-on edge with the right side of the work facing.

Purl the next 5 rows to give a garter stitch ridge. Work even in normal stockinette stitch until the back is 19½(19½, 19¾, 20½, 20½, 21)" (49.5[49.5, 50.5, 52, 52, 53.5]cm) long.

Shape shoulders

Next row: Knit to the last 3(3, 3, 3, 3, 4) stitches, wt.

Next row: Purl to the last 3(3, 3, 3, 3, 4) stitches, wt.

Next row: Knit to the last 6(6, 6, 7, 7, 8) stitches, wt.

Next row: Purl to the last 6(6, 6, 7, 7, 8) stitches, wt.

Next row: Knit to the last 9(9, 9, 11, 11, 12) stitches, wt.

Next row: Purl to the last 9(9, 9, 11, 11, 12) stitches, wt.

Next row: Knit to the last 12(11, 12, 15, 15, 16) stitches, wt.

Next row: Purl to the end of the row.

Bind off, working wraps with the stitches they wrap.

Left front

Cast on 27(31, 34, 37, 41, 44) stitches using size 9 (5.5mm) needles. Work 6 rows in garter stitch. Change to size 10½ (6.5mm) needles, and keeping the last 4 stitches of right-side rows and the first 4 stitches of wrong-side rows in garter stitch, work 4 rows.

Work the left edge of jacket and pocket lining: Knit 6 stitches, place the remaining 21(25, 28, 31, 35, 38) stitches onto a holder, cast on 14(14, 17, 17, 17, 17) stitches. You now have 20(20, 23, 23, 23, 23) stitches on the needle. Work a further 3 rows in stockinette stitch, the right side of the front is now facing for next row. Begin the side increases. Increase at beginning of the row on the next and following 10th row, work increase 2 stitches in from the edge of the front (k2, m1, k to end). Work side edge of garment and pocket lining until 7.5" (19cm) long and the right side of the front is facing, place stitches on a holder and return to remaining front stitches. Work even on these stitches, working the first and last 4 stitches of each row in garter stitch (in order to make pocket border as well as keeping continuity of garter stitch button band) until piece matches length of pocket lining, right side facing for the next row.

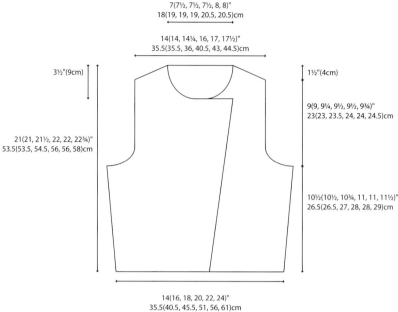

7(7½, 7½, 7½, 8, 8)"
18(19, 19, 19, 20.5, 20.5)cm

14(14, 14¼, 16, 17, 17½)"
35.5(35.5, 36, 40.5, 43, 44.5)cm

3½"(9cm)

1½"(4cm)

9(9, 9¼, 9½, 9½, 9¾)"
23(23, 23.5, 24, 24, 24.5)cm

21(21, 21½, 22, 22, 22¾)"
53.5(53.5, 54.5, 56, 56, 58)cm

10½(10½, 10¾, 11, 11, 11½)"
26.5(26.5, 27, 28, 28, 29)cm

14(16, 18, 20, 22, 24)"
35.5(40.5, 45.5, 51, 56, 61)cm

Join pocket lining to rest of front: Place pocket lining stitches onto a needle and k8, place pocket lining stitches behind stitches for rest of front and work over the next 14(14, 17, 17, 17, 17) stitches knitting together one stitch from each piece, k to the end of the row. Work in stockinette stitch from now on, increasing on every 10th row at the side edge of the front until there are 31(35, 38, 41, 45, 48) stitches, work even until the front matches the back to armhole shaping 10½(10½, 10¾, 11, 11, 11½)" (26.5[26.5, 27, 28, 28, 29]cm) with the right side facing for the next row.

X-Small: Bind off 2 stitches at the beginning of the next row, and 1 stitch on the next 2 following right-side rows.

Small, Medium, Large, X-Large, XX-Large: Bind off 3(3, 3, 3, 4) stitches at the beginning of the next row, then 2(2, 2, 2, 3) on the next right-side row, 1(1, 1, 2, 2) on the next, 1(1, 1, 1, 2) on the next, and then 1 stitch on the next 1(3, 3, 5, 4) right-side rows.

Work even until the front is 14¼(14¼, 14½, 15, 15, 15½)" (36[36, 37, 38, 38, 39.5]cm) from the cast-on edge with the right side of the work facing. Purl the next 5 rows to give a garter stitch ridge, BUT keep the 4 edge stitches in knit garter stitch (i.e., purl to the last 4 stitches, k4, and on the next row k4, then purl the rest of the stitches). Work even in stockinette stitch until the front measures 17½(17½, 18, 18½, 18½, 19¼)" (44.5[44.5, 45.5, 47, 47, 49]cm), with the wrong side of the front facing for the neck shaping:

Next row: Bind off 7(8, 8, 8, 8, 8) stitches at the beginning of the row, then 4(4, 4, 4, 5, 5) stitches at the beginning of the next wrong-side row, then 2(2, 2, 2, 2, 2) stitches on the following wrong-side row, and 1(1, 1, 1, 1, 1) stitch at the beginning of the next wrong-side row. Work even for 3 rows, then bind off 1 stitch at the beginning of the next wrong-side row. 12(11, 12, 15, 15, 16) stitches.

Work even until the front is 19½(19½, 19¾, 20½, 20½, 21)" (49.5[49.5, 50.5, 52, 52, 53.5]cm) long with the wrong side facing for the next row. Shape shoulders:

Next row: Purl to the last 3(3, 3, 3, 3, 4) stitches, wt.

Next row: Knit.

Next row: Purl to the last 6(6, 6, 7, 7, 8) stitches, wt.

Next row: Knit.

Next row: P to the last 9(9, 9, 11, 11, 12) stitches, wt.

Next row: Knit.

Next row: Purl across all stitches, purling wraps with the stitches they wrap. Bind off all stitches.

Right front

Cast on 24(28, 31, 34, 38, 41) stitches using size 9 (5.5mm) needles. Work 2 rows garter stitch.

Next row: Work first buttonhole. K6, yo, k2tog, k to end. Work 3 more rows garter

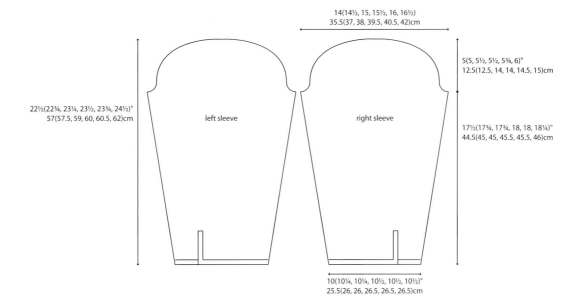

14(14½, 15, 15½, 16, 16½)"
35.5(37, 38, 39.5, 40.5, 42)cm

left sleeve

right sleeve

5(5, 5½, 5½, 5¾, 6)"
12.5(12.5, 14, 14, 14.5, 15)cm

22½(22¾, 23¼, 23½, 23¾, 24½)"
57(57.5, 59, 60, 60.5, 62)cm

17½(17¾, 17¾, 18, 18, 18¼)"
44.5(45, 45, 45.5, 45.5, 46)cm

10(10¼, 10¼, 10½, 10½, 10½)"
25.5(26, 26, 26.5, 26.5, 26.5)cm

stitch, change to size 10½ (6.5mm) needles and continue in stockinette stitch, keeping the first 4 stitches of the right side in garter stitch. Work 4 rows even, begin buttonhole band shaping and pocket on the next row.

Next row: k4, m1, k18(18, 21, 21, 21, 21), turn. Leave remaining stitches on a holder for side edge and pocket lining.

Next row (wrong side): K4, p to last 4 stitches, k4. Continue as set with 4 stitch garter stitch border for buttonhole and pocket bands, AT THE SAME TIME, increase 1 stitch after buttonhole band stitches (k4, m1) on the following 5th right-side row, and every 6th right-side row after that, and AT THE SAME TIME, work buttonhole 5" (12.5cm) up from garter stitch hem. Work buttonhole: K6, yo, k2tog, k to end. Work pocket stitches until pocket matches pocket depth on left front, place stitches on a holder. Return to 6 stitches left on holder for side edge and pocket lining, slip them back onto size 10½ (6.5mm) needle with the right side facing, rejoin yarn, cast on 14(14, 17, 17, 17, 17) stitches, knit across these, and then across the 6 stitches on the needle.

Next row: K4, p to end. Work as set, increase 1 stitch at side edge on following 3rd right-side row (knit to last 2 stitches, m1, k2), and then on every following 10th right-side row. When the side edge and pocket lining matches the pocket front with the right side facing, join the two pieces together. Slip the pocket front stitches from the holder back to a size 10½ (6.5mm) needle.

Next row: K9(9, 12, 12, 12, 12), place pocket lining stitches behind pocket front stitches, and knit across the next 14(14, 17, 17, 17, 17) stitches knitting them together, k to end. Continue in stockinette st, increasing at side edge (end of right-side rows) as set on every 10th row and also at center-front edge on every 6th row as set (k4, m1, k to end) AND ALSO WORKING BUTTONHOLE AS SET every 5" (12.5cm) until

front matches back to armhole shaping 10½(10½, 10¾, 11, 11, 11½)" (26.5 [26.5, 27, 28, 28, 29]cm) with the wrong side facing for the next row. Shape armholes, AND AT THE SAME TIME keep the continuity of the center-front increases as set already:

X-Small: Bind off 2 stitches at the beginning of the next row, and 1 stitch on the next 2 following wrong-side rows.

Small, Medium, Large, X-Large, XX-Large: Bind off 3(3, 3, 3, 4) stitches at the beginning of the next row, then 2(2, 2, 2, 3) on the next wrong-side row, 1(1, 1, 2, 2) on the next, 1(1, 1, 1, 2) on the next, and then 1 stitch on the next 1(3, 3, 5, 4) wrong-side rows.

Work even until the front is 14¼(14¼, 14½, 15, 15, 15½)" (36[36, 37, 38, 38, 39.5]cm) from the cast-on edge with the right side of the work facing, keeping continuity of the increases at the center-front. Purl the next 5 rows to give a garter stitch ridge, BUT keep the 4 edge stitches in knit garter stitch (i.e., k4, purl to the end of the row, and on the next row purl to the last 4 stitches, k4). Work even in stockinette stitch until you are ready to work the final buttonhole. Work 2 button-holes on this row:

Next row: *K6, yo, k2tog, repeat from * once, k to the end of the row. Work even until the front measures 17½(17½, 18, 18½, 18½, 19¼)" (44.5[44.5, 45.5, 47, 47, 49]cm), with the wrong side of the front facing for the neck shaping:

Next row: P20(20, 20, 23, 24, 25), turn. Leave remaining stitches on a holder for neckband.

Next row: Bind off 4(4, 4, 4, 5, 5) stitches, k to the end of the row.

Next row: Purl.

Next row: Bind off 2(2, 2, 2, 2, 2) stitches, k to the end of the row.

Next row: Cast off 1(1, 1, 1, 1, 1) stitch, k to the end of the row. Work 4 rows even, Next row (right side): Bind off 1(1, 1, 1, 1, 1) stitch, k to the end of the row. 12(11, 12, 15, 15, 16) stitches. Work even until right front matches back to start of shoulder shaping 19½(19½, 19¾, 20½, 20½, 21)" (49.5[49.5, 50.5, 52, 52, 53.5]cm) long with the right side facing for the next row.

Shape shoulders

Next row: Knit to the last 3(3, 3, 3, 3, 4) stitches, wt.

Next row: Purl to the end of the row.

Next row: Knit to the last 6(6, 6, 7, 7, 8) stitches, wt.

Next row: Purl to the end of the row.

Next row: Knit to the last 9(9, 9, 11, 11, 12) stitches, wt.

Next row: Purl to the end of the row.

Next row: Knit across all stitches, knitting the wraps with the stitches they wrap.

Next row: Bind off all stitches.

Sleeves

Left sleeve, 1st cuff piece

Cast on 24(25, 25, 26, 26, 26) stitches using size 9 (5.5mm) needles. Work 2 rows garter stitch, make buttonhole:

Next row: K2, yo, k2tog, k to the end of the row. Work 3 more rows garter stitch, change to size 10½ (6.5mm) needles and keeping the first 4 stitches of each right-side row and the last 4 stitches of each wrong-side row in garter stitch, work 16 rows stockinette stitch, increase 1 stitch at the end of 9th row (k22[23, 23, 24, 24, 24] m1, k2). Put these stitches on a spare needle.

Left sleeve, 2nd cuff piece

Cast on 13(14, 14, 15, 15, 15) stitches using size 9 (5.5mm) needles and work 6 rows of garter stitch. Change to size 10½ (6.5mm) needles and keeping the last 4 stitches of right-side rows and the first 4 stitches of wrong-side rows in garter stitch, work 16 rows stockinette stitch, increase 1 stitch at the beginning of the 9th row (k2, m1, k11[12, 12, 13, 13, 13]).

Join cuffs

Knit across first 10(11, 11, 12, 12, 12) stitches of the 2nd part of the cuff, now hold spare needle in front of the remaining 4 stitches with the 4 garter stitches of each piece overlapping, put the right-hand needle through the 1st stitch on the spare needle, then through the next stitch on the left-hand needle, knit these 2 stitches together. Repeat for the next 3 stitches, continue over remaining stitches as normal. 35(37, 37, 39, 39, 39) stitches. Continue in stockinette stitch, increase**:

X-Small, Small, Medium, and Large: 1 stitch at each end of 19th and every following 10th row until there are 47(49, 51, 53) stitches, work even until sleeve measures 17½(17¾, 17¾, 18)" (44.5[45, 45, 45.5]cm) from the cast-on edge.

X-Large, XX-Large: Increase 1 stitch at each end of the 19th, then *every following 6th then every following 8th row, repeat from * until there are 55(57) stitches. Work even until the sleeve measures 18(18¼)" (45.5[46]cm) from the cast-on edge. Increase row: K2, m1, k to last 2 stitches, m1, k2.

Shape sleeve cap

Bind off 3 stitches at the beginning of the next 2 rows, then 2 stitches at the beginning of the next 2 rows, then 1 stitch at the beginning of the next 18(18, 20, 20, 22, 24) rows. Bind off 2 stitches at the beginning of the next 2 rows, then 3 stitches at the beginning of the following 2 rows, bind off the remaining 9(11, 11, 13, 13, 13) stitches.

Right sleeve, 1st cuff piece

Cast on 24(25, 25, 26, 26, 26) stitches using size 9 (5.5mm) needles. Work 2 rows of garter stitch, make buttonhole:

Next row: Knit to the last 4 stitches, yo, k2tog, k2. Work 3 more rows in garter stitch, change to size 10½ (6.5mm) needles and keeping the last 4 stitches of each right-side row and the first 4 stitches of each wrong-side row in garter stitch, work 16 rows stockinette stitch, increase 1 stitch at the beginning of the 9th row (k2, m1, k22[22, 23, 24, 24, 24]). Put these stitches on a spare needle.

Right sleeve, 2nd cuff piece

Cast on 13(14, 14, 15, 15, 15) stitches using size 9 (5.5mm) needles and work 6 rows of garter stitch. Change to size 10½ (6.5mm) needles and keeping the first 4 stitches of right-side rows and the last 4 stitches of wrong-side rows in garter stitch, work 16 rows stockinette stitch, increase 1 stitch at end of the 9th row (k11[12, 12, 13, 13, 13] m1, k2).

Join cuffs

Knit across the first 21(22, 22, 23, 23, 23) stitches of the 1st part of the cuff, now hold the needle with the 2nd part of cuff behind the remaining 4 stitches with the 4 garter stitches overlapping, put the right-hand needle through the 1st stitch on the left-hand needle, then through the 1st stitch on the spare needle, knit these 2 stitches together. Repeat for the next 3 stitches, continue over the remaining stitches as normal. 35(37, 37, 39, 39, 39) stitches. Work as for left sleeve from **.

Neckband

Join shoulder seams. With the right side of the jacket facing and size 9 (5.5mm) needles, knit across the stitches left on the holder from the right front neck, * knit up 16(16, 16, 16, 16, 16) stitches from the right front neck, 23(25, 25, 25, 27, 27) stitches across the back neck and 23(24, 24, 24, 25, 25) stitches from the left front neck. 62(65, 65, 65, 68, 68) stitches picked up, plus the stitches from the holder (the exact total is not important here, it may be different from knitter to knitter because of variations in row gauge affecting the number of increases made in the right front. On the size small shown in the picture at right, there were 19 stitches on the holder, giving a total of 84 stitches for the neckband). Work 6 rows in garter stitch, bind off.

Finishing

Set in sleeves, sew side and sleeve seams. Sew on buttons, sew in all ends.

Skill level: Easy.

Size: Finished scarf is approximately 42" (106.5cm) long and 8" (20.5cm) wide.

Materials:

5 skeins Treenway Silks Bombyx Silk 20/60, 100% silk [3½ oz (100g), 326yd (301m)], 1 each in Truffle, Evening Spirit, Platinum, Mermaid's Tears, and Ice Poppy. fine

Size 4 (3.5mm) needles.

Gauge: 24½ stitches and 32 rows to 4" (10cm) over stockinette stitch on size 4 (3.5mm) needles.

Cast on 63 stitches using size 4(3.5mm) needles and Truffle. Knit 1 row as a foundation row.

Begin chevron in garter stitch pattern:

Row 1: K1, ssk, * k9, sl2, k1, p2sso, repeat from * to the last 12 stitches, end k9, k2tog, k1.

Row 2: K1 * p1, k4, (k1, yo, k1) in the next stitch, k4, repeat from * to the last 2 stitches, p1, k1.

Repeat these 2 rows for 6"(15cm), using the stripe pattern as detailed below.

Now change to Platinum to work the stockinette stitch version of the pattern for 6" (15cm):

Row 1: As before.

Row 2: K5, p1, *(p1, yo, p1) in the next stitch, p9, repeat from * to the last 7 stitches, (p1,yo, p1) in the next stitch, p1, k5.

Always work the stockinette stitch section in Platinum.

Work this section of pattern for 6" (15cm).

Repeat these 2 sections twice more, then work the garter stitch section once more, bind off.

Finishing

Sew in all ends, then add 2½" (5cm) Platinum tassels to each end of the scarf.

Stripe sequence
Work 2 rows each of Truffle, Evening Spirit, Mermaid's Tears, Ice Poppy, Evening Spirit, Truffle, Ice Poppy, Mermaid's Tears. 16 rows in total, then 4 rows each of Truffle, Ice Poppy, Evening Spirit, Truffle, Mermaid's Tears, Evening Spirit, Ice Poppy. The whole entire sequence is 48 rows, if you end the first section of the garter stitch chevron at (say) the first 2-row Mermaid's Tears stripe, start the section on the 2 rows of Ice Poppy that come after it in the sequence.

Lizzie's Coffee and Walnut Cake

FROM SMOKEY JOE'S TRUCK STOP CAFÉ

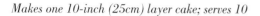

Makes one 10-inch (25cm) layer cake; serves 10

CAKE LAYERS

¾ cup (150 grams) sugar

1 stick (113 grams) unsalted butter, softened

4 large eggs

3 oz (75 grams) unsweetened cocoa powder

1 cup (240ml) whole milk

2 cups plus 2 tablespoons (300 grams) self-rising flour

To make the cake layers, preheat the oven to 350°F (175°C). Grease three 10-inch (25cm) baking pans.

Beat the butter and sugar together in an electric mixer until creamy in texture. Add the eggs and cocoa powder and mix until smooth. If the cake mixture looks dry and stiff, add add a few tablespoons (30 ml) of milk.

Mix the flour into the beaten egg mixture until just combined. The batter will be runny.

Divide the batter evenly among the prepared baking pans. Bake for 25 minutes until a metal skewer inserted in the center comes out dry. Unmold and cool on a wire rack.

FILLING AND TOPPING

2 quarts (1.9l) heavy cream

5 tablespoons (32.5g) instant Cappuccino mix

One 14-ounce (420ml) can condensed milk

12 tablespoons (120ml) Tia Maria* or brandy

Confectioner's sugar as needed

5 tablespoons (32.5g) unsweetened cocoa powder

20 walnuts, halved

½ cup (42.5g) chocolate shavings

To make the filling, mix the heavy cream with the instant cappuccino mix and then whisk until it is nearly forming peaks. Add the condensed milk and half of the Tia Maria. If the consistency is too soft to hold up the layers of cake, add confectioner's sugar, one tablespoon (15ml) at a time, to thicken the mixture until it is stiff.

When the sponge cakes are cool alternate layers of cake with the cream filling mixture.

Sprinkle the cream filling over the cake, adding the rest of the Tia Maria at the end.

Decorate with walnut halves and chocolate.

Smokey Joe's Truck Stop Café

The café featured in this chapter is Smokey Joe's, situated just off the A30 (at the A3047 intersection) in southwest England. It was originally opened as a steakhouse and was popular with late-night revelers after various local nightclubs had closed for the evening. Over the years it began to pick up business as a roadside diner and for the last five years has been run solely as a truck stop, opening each day from 7 a.m. to 10 p.m. Smokey Joe's specializes in traditional home cooking, and most of its produce is sourced locally. If you are really hungry, try the huge all-day breakfast, and if you have a sweet tooth, try the deliciously "naughty but nice" coffee and walnut cake.

chapter six

ROSE POUCHONG TEA

Rose pouchong is a pure black China tea with the addition of rose petals. The tea is grown in the Guangdong Province of China and on the island of Taiwan, formerly known as Formosa. The leaves of this tea are large and are scattered with fresh pink rose petals, which infuse a natural, perfumed rose oil into the tea leaves as they dry.

Rose pouchong is traditionally served in the late afternoon or early evening, and it should only be accompanied by the lightest of foods, so as not to spoil its exquisite taste. The tea should be taken without milk, but a slice of lime and a little sugar can enhance the delicate flavor.

Rose pouchong tea tastes best when consumed from fine porcelain tea cups. It is said that when you drink from a delicate china tea cup, the slightly curved "lip" sends the tea to a different part of the tongue—hence the difference in flavor.

Vessels for making and drinking tea evolved in China from bronze through stoneware to porcelain. From the end of the seventeenth century, porcelain teapots were exported to Europe in the ships that brought the tea. Most of these teapots were painted in blue and white. When European potteries began to produce teapots, they were inspired by these Chinese designs.

Bone china was invented by Josiah Spode in England around 1800. The addition of animal bone to the kaolin produced china ware with a high degree of translucency, whiteness, and strength.

In the same way that tea drinking has varied throughout history from the refined to the popular, the history of knitting has encompassed the use of techniques, traditions, and materials that vary enormously from the mundane to the exotic. Today, the most sophisticated array of yarns is available—alpaca, merino, silk, and bamboo—and are all used by the twenty-first-century knitter.

Knitting with fine yarns, accompanied by a delicate china cup of rose pouchong tea. What an exquisite combination!

Skill level: Intermediate.

Size: S(M, L).

Finished Bust: 42(46, 50¼)" (106.5[117, 127.5]cm).

Materials:

5(6, 7) skeins Blue Sky Alpacas Suri Merino, 60% Baby Suri, 40% Merino Wool [3½ oz (100g) 164yd (150m)] Snow. (4) medium Size 6 (4mm) 16 and 40" (100cm) circular needles and size 7 (4.5mm) straight needles.

Gauge: 30½ stitches and 28 rows to 4" (10cm) over cable pattern on size 7 (4.5mm) needles.

Back

Cast on 160(176, 192) stitches using size 7 (4.5mm) needles. Work in cable pattern from chart for 28 rows, ending with the right side of the work facing. Keeping pattern correct, start shaping:

Bind off 1 stitch at the beginning of the next 4 rows, work 2 rows even, *1 stitch at the beginning of the next 2 rows, work 2 rows even *, repeat from * twice more, 1 stitch at the beginning of the next 10 rows, repeat from * to * once, 1 stitch at the beginning of the next 12 rows, bind off 2 stitches at the beginning of the next 6 rows, then 1 stitch at the beginning of the next 8 rows, and 2 stitches at the beginning of the next 2 rows. 102(118, 134) stitches. Shape shoulders:

Bind off 7(10, 13) stitches at the beginning of the next 3 rows, pattern 9(11, 13), turn.

Next row: P2tog, work in pattern to the end of the row. Bind off the remaining 8(10, 12) stitches. Rejoin yarn to the remaining stitches, bind off the central 56 stitches, work in pattern to the end of the row.

Next row: Bind off 7(10, 13) stitches, work in pattern to the end of the row.

Next row: P2tog, work in pattern to the end of the row. Bind off the remaining 8(10, 12) stitches.

Left front

Cast on 28(36, 44) stitches. Work the foundation row from the chart starting at stitch 28(36, 44). Continue in cable pattern from the chart, keeping the right-side edge of the work straight (side edge of Capelet), cast on at the beginning of each wrong-side row (the center-front edge) 5 stitches 11 times, 4 stitches twice, 3 stitches once. Now decrease at the side edge AT THE SAME TIME as increasing at the center-front edge.

Decreases, all worked at the beginning of right-side rows: Bind off 1 stitch at the beginning of the next 2 rows, work 2 rows even, *1 stitch at the beginning of the next row, work 2 rows even *, repeat from * twice more, 1 stitch at the beginning of the next 5 rows, repeat from * to * once, 1 stitch at the beginning of the next 2 rows. Start front neck shaping.

Increases at the center-front edge: 3 stitches once, 2 stitches 16 times.

Bind off 1 stitch at the beginning of the next row, pattern 55(63, 71) stitches, turn. Continue to work side edge shaping as follows, and AT THE SAME TIME, decrease at neck edge:

Neck decreases (all worked at the beginning of wrong-side rows): Bind off 4 stitches twice, then 2 stitches 4 times, *work 3 rows even, bind off 1 stitch, repeat from * once. Work even at neck edge now.

Shoulder decreases, all worked at the beginning of right-side rows: Bind off 1 stitch at the beginning of the next 4 rows, bind off 2 stitches at the beginning of the next 3 rows, then 1 stitch at the beginning of the next 4 rows, and 2 stitches at the beginning of the next row. Bind off 7(10, 13) stitches at the beginning of the next 2 right-side rows, bind off the remaining 8(10, 12) stitches.

Rejoin yarn to the remaining stitches, bind off the first 24 stitches, work in pattern to the end.

Next row: Resume increases as follows, BUT AT THE SAME TIME, work neck decreases as given below. Work 1 row even, cast on 2 stitches at the beginning of the next 6 wrong-side rows, work 3 rows even, cast on 2 stitches, work 3 rows even, cast on 1 stitch. Work 1 row even, start shoulder shaping. Cast off 1 stitch at the beginning of the next row, work 1 row even, cast off 2 stitches at the beginning of the next row. Bind off 7(10, 13) stitches at the beginning of the next 2 wrong-side rows, bind off the remaining 8(10, 12) stitches.

Neck decreases, all worked at the beginning of right-side rows: Bind off 4 stitches twice, then 2 stitches 4 times, *work 3 rows even, bind off 1 stitch, repeat from * once. Work even at neck edge now.

Right front

Cast on 28(36, 44) stitches. Work the foundation row from the chart starting at stitch 21(13, 5). Continue in cable pattern from the chart, keeping the left-side edge of the work straight (side edge of Capelet), cast on at the beginning of each right-side row (the center-front edge) 5 stitches 10 times. Work even at this edge for 5 rows. Now begin decreases at the side edge AT THE SAME TIME as decreasing at the center-front edge.

Decreases, all worked at the beginning of right-side rows: Bind off 4 stitches twice, 3 stitches twice, and 2 stitches at the beginning of the next 21 right-side rows. * Work 3 rows even, bind off 2 stitches, repeat from * once. Work 2 rows even. Decreases, all worked at the beginning of wrong-side rows (side edge): Bind off 1 stitch at the beginning of the next 2 rows, work 2 rows even, *1 stitch at the beginning of the next row, work 2 rows even *, repeat from * twice more, 1 stitch at the beginning of the next 5 rows, repeat from * to * once, 1 stitch at the beginning of the next 6 rows, bind off 2 stitches at the beginning of the next 3 rows, then 1 stitch at the beginning of the next 4 rows, and 2 stitches at the beginning of the next row.

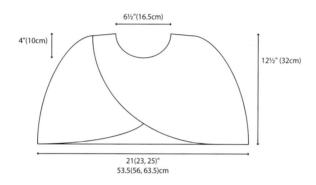

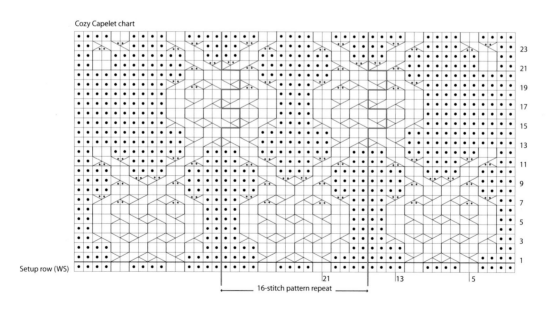

Cozy Capelet chart

Setup row (WS)

16-stitch pattern repeat

• Purl on the right side, knit on the wrong side.

Slip 2 stitches onto a cable needle and hold at the back of the work, k2, k2 from the cable needle.

Slip 2 stitches onto a cable needle and hold at the front of the work, k2, k2 from the cable needle.

Slip 2 stitches onto a cable needle and hold at the back of the work, k2, p2 from the cable needle.

Slip 2 stitches onto a cable needle and hold at the front of the work, p2, k2 from the cable needle.

Shape shoulder:

Bind off 4(6, 10) stitches at the beginning of the next row, 7(10, 13) stitches at the beginning of the next wrong-side row, bind off the remaining 8(10, 12) stitches on the next wrong-side row.

Sew the side seams and shoulders of the Capelet, positioning the left front just over the right front at the shoulder. With the right side of the Capelet facing and the size 6 (4mm) circular needle, pick up and knit 130(136, 142) down the left front from the right shoulder to the side seam, 121(131, 141) along the bottom of the back, and 64(68, 72) up from the side seam to the last of the 5 cast-on stitches of the right front. 315(335, 355) stitches. Work 5 rows in k1, p1 rib, bind off in rib. Sew the rib edging down to the top of the right shoulder, and catch the ribbing at the edge of the right front (and the cast-off edge of the right front) neatly underneath the left front.

Neck (all sizes)

With the right side of the Capelet facing and the shorter size 6 (4mm) circular needle, pick up and knit 23 down from the left shoulder to the middle of the front neck, 16 across the front neck, placing a marker between the 8th and 9th stitches picked up here at the very center front of the neck, 23 up the right-front neck and 50 across the back neck. 112 stitches. Join into a round and work 1" (2.5cm) in k2, p2 ribbing, the marker should sit between 2 knit stitches. After 1" (2.5cm), work around to the marker, turn and work back and forth in rows from now on for 3½" (9cm). Bind off in rib.

Finishing

Sew in all ends.

Skill level: Easy / Intermediate.

Size: 60" (152.5cm) long and 14¾" (37.5cm) wide.

Materials:

10 skeins Blue Sky Alpacas Suri Merino, 60% Baby Suri, 40% Merino Wool [3½ oz (100g) 164yd (150m)] Fog. (4) medium
Size 6 (4mm) 40" (100cm) circular needle and size 7 (4.5mm) straight needles.

Gauge: 20 stitches and 27 rows to 4" (10cm) stockinette stitch on size 7 (4.5mm) needles.

Left side of wrap

Cast on 36 stitches using size 7 (4.5mm) needles.

Row 1: K10, p1, *k4, p1, repeat from * twice more, k10.

Row 2: Work the stitches as they face you.

Row 3: Cast on 4 stitches, work from the chart for the 1st cabled row.

Row 4: Cast on 4 stitches, work the rest of the stitches as they face you.

Continue following the chart for placement of cables and increases, finishing the increases on the 22nd row. 92 stitches. Work even for a further 22 rows.

Row 45: Pattern 34, slip the next 30 stitches onto a holder for the pocket top, pattern across 30 stitches from one pocket lining, work in pattern to the end.

Continue now with cable pattern as set until 204 rows have been worked and the piece is approximately 29½" (75cm) long. Put stitches on a holder ready for grafting when the 2nd piece is finished.

Right side of wrap

Work as for the left side until 44 rows have been worked. Place pocket on the 45th row: Pattern 28, slip the next 30 stitches onto a holder for the pocket top, pattern across 30 stitches from the remaining pocket lining, work in pattern to the end of the row. Work until piece matches left side.

Using Kitchener stitch, graft the two pieces together.

Hood

Cast on 112 stitches using size 7 (4.5mm) needles. Work cables from the chart as for the wrap, but include 1 extra repeat of the 10-stitch cable panel (marked in blue) on each side of the wrap repeats. Work even until the hood is 14¼" (36cm). Fold the hood in half and Kitchener stitch the top edges together. Sew hood to wrap, setting center of hood to the grafted seam on the wrap.

Edging

Starting at the center-back hem with the right side of the wrap facing and using the size 6 (4mm) circular needle, pick up and knit 122 stitches from the center-back to the start of the hem curve, 29 stitches around the curve, 28 stitches along the cast-on edge, 29 stitches around the curve, 80 stitches along the front edge to the hood seam, pick up and mark 1 stitch from the point at which the hood is joined to the wrap, pick up 65 stitches up the right front of the hood, 64 down the left front of hood, pick up and mark 1 stitch from the point at which the hood joins the wrap, 80 stitches down the right front edge, 29 stitches around the curve, 28 stitches from the cast-on edge, 29 stitches around the curve, and 121 along the left back edge to the center-back. 706 stitches.

Left side of Snug Hooded Wrap
Refer to the written pattern for the pocket placement for the right side of the wrap.

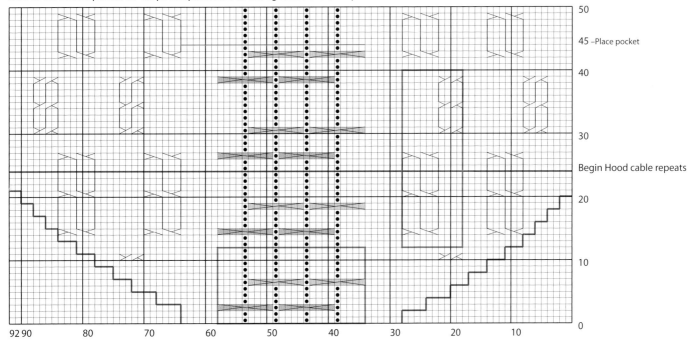

Join into a round and work 1 round in k1, p1 rib. The two marked stitches on either side of the hood should be knit stitches.

Round 2: Rib to 2 stitches before the marked stitch on the right side of the hood. K1, sl 1 p-wise, psso, k the marked stitch, k2tog. Rib to 2 stitches before the 2nd marked stitch, repeat these decreases. Rib the rest of the round. 702 stitches. Work 1 more round even, 1 more working decreases as on the 2nd round. Bind off in rib.

Pocket lining (make 2)

Cast on 30 stitches using size 7 (4.5mm) needles. Work 28 rows in stockinette stitch, place stitches on a holder until needed.

Pocket tops

Left side: Using size 6 (4mm) circular needle, knit across the 30 stitches held for the pocket top, decreasing 8 stitches across the large central cable: K2tog 9 times, k13. 21 stitches. Work 5 rows p1, k1 rib, bind off in rib. Slip stitch the edges of pocket top to wrap.

Right side: Using size 6 (4mm) circular needle, knit across the 30 stitches held for the pocket top, decreasing 8 stitches across the large central cable: K13, (k2tog) 9 times. Work as for left side.

Finishing

Sew in all ends, make a tassel, and sew to the point of the hood.

Skill level: Easy.

Size: to fit a 19" (48.5cm) diameter teapot.

Materials:
1 skein 2oz (56g) of Treenway Silks Bombyx Silk 20/60, 100% silk [3½ oz (100g), 326yd (301m)]. **①** superfine
in Ice Poppy, Lapis Lazuli, Mermaid's Tears, Persian Night, Platinum, and Truffle.
Size 3 (3.25mm) needles.

Gauge: 28 stitches and 36 rows to 4" (10cm) over stockinette stitch on size 3 (3.25mm) needles.

Note: Do not cut yarns at the edges, carry each one up the side of the work.

Stripe sequence:

Color 1: Mermaid's Tears

Color 2: Truffle

Color 3: Persian Night

Color 4: Ice Poppy

Color 5: Lapis Lazuli

Color 6: Platinum

Cast on 46 stitches using size 3 (3.25mm) needles and color 1.

Knit 1 row.

Next row: P34, wt.

Next row: K34.

Next row: Purl all stitches, purling the wrap with the wrapped stitch. Change to color 2.

Purl 1 row.

Next row: K34, wt.

Next row: P34.

Next row: Knit all stitches, knitting the wrap with the wrapped stitch. Change to color 3.

Knit 1 row.

Next row: P34, wt.

Next row: K34.

Next row: Purl all stitches, purling the wrap with the wrapped stitch. Change to color 4.

Purl 1 row.

Next row: K34, wt.

Next row: P34.

Next row: Knit all stitches, knitting the wrap with the wrapped stitch. Change to color 5.

Knit 1 row.

Next row: P34, wt.

Next row: K34.

Next row: Purl all stitches, purling the wrap with the wrapped stitch. Change to color 6.

Purl 1 row.

Next row: K34, wt.

Next row: P34.

Next row: Knit all stitches, knitting the wrap with the wrapped stitch. Change to color 1.

Repeat these 24 rows twice more, then repeat the 1st 3 rows again with color 1, bind off. Make another piece the same.

Finishing

Sew the two pieces together, leaving spaces for the spout and handle of your teapot. Gather up the side edge of the knitting where the colors have been carried up and fasten securely. Make a fat tassel of all colors mixed together and attach to this gathered end.

Skill level: Easy.

Size: Finished Cozies are approximately 4½" (11.5cm) high, excluding the tassel.

Materials:

1 skein of Treenway Silks Bombyx Silk 20/60, 100% silk [3½ oz (100g), 326yd (301m)] in Electric Dijon, Evening Spirit, Flamingo, Mermaid's Tears, Platinum, Pomegranate, Shelly Belly. **(1)** superfine
Size 3 (3.25mm) needles.

Gauge: 28 stitches and 36 rows to 4" (10cm) over stockinette stitch on size 3 (3.25mm) needles.

Note: Do not cut yarns at the edges, carry each one up the side of the work.

Cast on 26 stitches using size 3 (3.25mm) needles and color 1. Work 4 rows in stockinette stitch, beginning with a knit row. Change to color 2, work 4 rows in reverse stockinette stitch (begin with a purl row). Change to color 3, work 4 rows in stockinette stitch (begin with a knit row).

Repeat these 3 color, 4 row stripes of stockinette stitch and reverse stockinette stitch until 36 rows have been worked. Keeping stockinette and reverse stockinette stitch pattern correct, work 4 rows in color 4, then carry on with colors 1, 2, and 3 as before.

After 64 rows have been completed, bind off. Join cast-on edge to bound-off edge. Gather up the side edge of the knitting where the colors have been carried up and fasten securely. Make a fat tassel of colors 1, 2, and 3 mixed together and attach to this gathered end.

Colorways for the 4-color Cozies:

Cozy 1

Color 1: Pomegranate

Color 2: Flamingo

Color 3: Shelly Belly

Color 4: Electric Dijon

Cozy 2

Color 1: Truffle

Color 2: Platinum

Color 3: Evening Spirit

Color 4: Mermaid's Tears

Colorways for the 2-color Cozies:

The 2-color Cozies are knitted making each stripe 8 rows instead of 4. So knit 8 rows in stockinette stitch, then 8 rows in reverse stockinette stitch until you've knitted 64 rows. Finish as for the 4-color Cozies.

Cozy 1

Color 1: Mermaid's Tears

Color 2: Lapis Lazuli

Cozy 2

Color 1: Pomegranate

Color 2: Platinum

Skill level: Easy.

Size: The Purse is 9½" (24cm) long, excluding tassels.

Materials:
2oz (56g) of Treenway Silks Bombyx Silk 20/60, 100% silk [3½ oz (100g), 326yd (301m)]
in Pomegranate, Shelly Belly, Electric Dijon, Flamingo. superfine.
Metal ring for fastening (we used a piece of costume jewelry).
Size 3 (3.25mm) double-pointed needles.

Gauge: 28 stitches and 36 rows to 4" (10cm) over stockinette stitch on size 3 (3.25mm) needles.

Cast on 60 stitches with Pomegranate, leaving a long tail of yarn to draw these stitches up with later. Put 20 onto each of 3 needles and join into a round, being careful not to twist the stitches.

Round 1: K1, p1 around.

Round 2: P1, k1 around (this will make a seed stitch). Work these 2 rounds for 1" (2.5cm).

Work 2 rounds where you knit all stitches (stockinette stitch). Cut yarn.

Join in color Shelly Belly. Knit 1 round.

Openwork pattern round: *Yf, slip 1 k2tog, repeat from * around. Work this round for ½" (13mm). Work 1 round knitting all stitches. Cut yarn.

Change to Dijon, work ½" (13mm) in seed stitch as detailed previously. Now repeat the openwork pattern for ½" (13mm), then work 2 rounds where all the stitches are knitted, then work a further ½" (13mm) in the openwork pattern. Work 1 round where all the stitches are knitted. Cut yarn.

Join in Shelly Belly again and start to work backward and forward in rows, not rounds, now in stockinette stitch, so that you make an opening for the Purse. Work 2½" (5cm) this way. Cut yarn.

Join in Flamingo, and work in rounds again. Knit 2 rounds.

Next round: * K2tog, slip 1, yf, work from * around for 4 rounds. Cut yarn.

Join in Pomegranate and work 3 rounds of seed stitch. Work a further 1½" (4cm) of openwork pattern as just given for Flamingo. Cut yarn.

Join in Electric Dijon, work ½" (13mm) in seed stitch. Cut yarn, thread through all the stitches and draw up, fasten off securely. Run the cast-on tail thread through the cast-on edge, draw up and fasten securely.

Finishing

Sew in all ends. Make 2 tassels, one each in colors A and C. Slide the ring onto the purse, then attach a tassel to each end.

This type of elegant knitted silk purse was very popular in the Victorian and Edwardian eras. The tubular purse features tassels at each end as well as a slit in the middle so you can take your money in and out. When you slide the metal ring (bought at a jewelry store) below the slit, it holds the money in place. If you want to take your money out, you slide the ring above the slit.

Mini Meringues

FROM THE LIME TREE RESTAURANT

Makes 30 mini-meringues

6 large egg whites

1½ cups (300 grams) granulated sugar

2 cups (500 grams) heavy cream

½ pint raspberries

Confectioner's sugar for dusting

Preheat the oven to 212°F (100°C). Line a baking sheet with parchment paper.

Whisk the egg whites in an electric mixer until they form soft peaks. Gently whisk in the granulated sugar and whisk until you get a shine to the meringue.

Using a teaspoon, spoon the meringue mixture onto the parchment at least 1" (2.5cm) apart. Bake for 1 hour at 212°F (100°C). Lower the oven temperature to 180°F (80°C) and bake for 1 hour.

Allow the meringues to cool on the baking sheet.

Whisk the heavy cream until it forms soft peaks.

Split the meringues lengthwise and fill them with a little cream and four raspberries per meringue.

Dust with confectioner's sugar before serving.

The Lime Tree Restaurant

Trevelyan House
16 Chapel Street
Penzance, TR18 4AW

Website: *www.the-lime-tree.co.uk*
Telephone 011 44 1736332555
E-mail *info@the-lime-tree.co..uk*

The Lime Tree in Penzance is found on the first floor of a beautiful Georgian building that was built as a doctor's residence in the 1840s. It later became the site of a wine importation business and then a brewery company. In 1885 it was the home of the local *Telegraph* newspaper. Later on the building was used as a hotel.

Run by husband and wife team of Miki and Justin Ashton, the Lime Tree has already established a reputation for producing delicious, imaginative food, made with high-quality local ingredients. Justin's menus draw on eclectic influences from all over the world.

Abbreviations

Knitting abbreviations

B1 / B1K: Place bead. Bring yarn to the front of the work, push a bead right up to the right-hand needle, slip the next stitch purl-wise, take yarn to the back of the work and continue knitting. The bead should sit snugly in front of the stitch just slipped. The B1K abbreviation is used in the Flowerdew Evening Tank work in pattern to differentiate from the purl stitches with beads as described on the chart.

dec: Decrease.

g st: Garter stitch (every row k).

inc: Increase.

k: Knit.

K1B / P1B: Knit or purl stitch through back of loop (to twist the stitch).

k2tog / p2tog: Knit / purl the next 2 (or number specified) stitches together.

kfb / pfb: Knit or purl into front and back of the next stitch to make a stitch.

LH / RH: Left hand / right hand.

m1k/m1p: Pick up strand that lies between the stitch just worked and the next stitch, knit (or purl) into the back of it.

p: Purl.

p2sso: Pass 2 slipped stitches over.

pattern 2 together: Work 2 stitches together while continuing in pattern.

rev st st: Reverse stockinette (purl side is RS).

RS / WS: Right side / wrong side.

skpo: Slip one, knit one, pass the slipped stitch over.

sl 1 p-wise / k-wise: Slip the next stitch as if to purl / knit.

SQ1: Place sequin. Push the sequin right up to the back of the work. Knit the next stitch, but as you do so push the sequin through the stitch as you knit it. This makes the sequin lie flat on the front of the work, and is much easier to do than to explain!

ssk: Slip, slip knit—slip the next 2 stitches k-wise, place tip of LH needle into front of these two stitches and knit them together.

st st: Stockinette / stocking stitch.

wt: Wrap and turn. Bring yarn to front (if on a knit row) of work, slip the next stitch, take yarn to back of work, slip the wrapped stitch back to the left hand needle. Turn work. If on a purl row, take yarn to back of work, slip the next stitch, bring yarn to front of work, slip the wrapped stitch back to LH needle, turn work.

y2rn: Yarn twice around needle.

yb: Yarn back—take yarn to the back of the work.

yfwd: Yarn forward—bring yarn to the front of the work.

yo: Yarn over. Bring yarn from the back of the work, over needle to the front and to the back again.

Crochet abbreviations:

ch: Chain

sc: Single crochet

ss: Slip stitch

Stitch Glossary

I-cord: Cast on required number of stitches onto a double-pointed needle. *Without turning work, slide stitches onto right-hand end of needle, pull yarn around back of stitches and knit as usual. Repeat from * until cord is required length.

I-cord border: Pick up the appropriate number of stitches from the edge to be bordered using a circular needle. Pull needle through so that you are ready to work from the beginning of the picked up stitches (the RS of work will be facing you).
Work I-cord edging as follows:
On a separate needle cast on 2 stitches. Transfer them to the circular needle, holding the edge stitches. Now work as follows: * K1, slip1, yo, k1 (from edge stitches), pass the 2 slip stitches over (the slipped stitch and the yarn over). Replace the 2 stitches on the right-hand needle to the left-hand needle and rep from * to the end of stitches. The border can be eased around corners (e.g., on collars, blankets) by working the first 2 stitches only once or twice before then carrying on from *.

K1, p1 rib: Worked over any number of stitches and a 2-row repeat.
Row 1: K1, p1 to the end of the row.
Row 2: Work stitches as they face you, so if you ended the first row with a knit stitch, begin the second row with a purl stitch.

K2, p2 rib: Worked over a multiple of 2 stitches and a 2-row repeat.
Row 1: K2, p2 to the end of the row.
Row 2: Work stitches as they face you, so if you ended the first row with a p2, begin the second row with a k2.

Seed stitch: Worked over any number of stitches and a 2-row repeat.
Row 1: K1, p1 to the end of the row.
Row 2: Work stitches as you did on the first row, so if you ended the first row with a knit stitch, begin the second row with a knit stitch.

Stockinette stitch: Worked over any number of stitches and a 2-row repeat.
Row 1 (RS): Knit.
Row 2: Purl.

Kitchener stitch:
A method of grafting two sets of live stitches together. Holding each set of stitches on 2 separate needles, hold the wrong sides of the work together so that the knit sides of the two works are facing out. Use a long tail from one of your pieces, thread a tapestry needle and pass your needle through the first stitch of the forward needle as if to purl and pull the needle and yarn through. Then, keeping the working yarn and needle UNDER the needles, pass the needle through the first stitch of the back needle as if to knit.

Resources

Yarns

Blue Sky Alpacas, Inc.
P.O. Box 88
Cedar, MN 55011
Telephone (763) 753–5815
Website   www.blueskyalpacas.com
E-mail   info@blueskyalpacas.com

Karabella Yarns, Inc.
1201 Broadway
New York, NY 10001
Telephone (212) 684–2665
Website   www.karabellayarns.com
E-mail   info@karabellayarns.com

Lion Brand Yarn
135 Kero Road
Carlstadt, NJ 07072
Telephone (800) 258-YARN (9276) [Orders]
Website   www.lionbrand.com

Rowan Yarns/RYC
Westminster Fibers, Inc.
165 Ledge Street
Nashua, NH 03060
Telephone 1–800–445–9276
Website   www.knitrowan.com
E-mail   Mail@knitrowan.com

Treenway Silks
501 Musgrave Road
Salt Spring Island, BC
V8K 1V5
Canada
Telephone (250) 653–2345
Website   www.treenwaysilks.com
E-mail   silk@treenwaysilks.com

Tea Rooms

United Kingdom

All of the following U.K. tea rooms have been awarded the Tea Guild's Award of Excellence. You can explore more U.K. tea rooms by visiting www.tea.co.uk.

Badgers Tearooms
The Victoria Centre
Mostyn Street
Llandudno LL30 2RP
Telephone 011 44 1492871649
Website www.badgersgroup.co.uk/tearooms

Darcys Tea & Dining Rooms
52 Eastbank Street
Southport Merseyside PR8 1ES
Telephone 011 44 1704543290
Website www.darcystearooms.co.uk

Elizabeth Botham and Sons
35/39 Skinner Street
Whitby YO21 3AH
Telephone 011 44 1947602823
Website www.botham.co.uk

Juri's—The Olde Bakery Tea Shoppe
High Street
Winchcombe
Cheltenham GL54 5LJ
Telephone 011 44 1242602469
Website www.Juris-Tearoom.co.uk

The Lanesborough
Hyde Park Corner
Knightsbridge
London SW1X 7TA
Telephone 011 44 20 72595599
Website www.lanesborough.com

The Marshmallow Tearooms & Restaurant
High Street
Morton-in-Marsh
Gloucestershire GL56 0AT
Telephone 011 44 1608651536
Email sallyannwebb@tiscali.co.uk

Moggerhanger Park Tearooms
Moggerhanger Park
Park Road
Moggerhanger MK44 3RW
Telephone 011 44 1767641007
Website www.moggerhangerpark.com

Willow Tea Rooms
97 Buchanan Street
Glasgow G1 3HF
Telephone 011 44 1412045242
Website www.willowtearooms.co.uk

U.S.

The following U.S. tea rooms serve Afternoon Tea in the British tradition. You can find more tea rooms in your area by visiting www.greattearoomsofamerica.com and www.teamap.com.

Northeast

AntiquiTeas Tearoom
217 Rockingham Road
Rt. 28 Londonderry, NH 03053
Telephone 603–432–7979
Website www.antiquiteastearoom.com

Harney & Sons Fine Teas
Main Street, The Railroad Plaza;
Millerton, NY
Telephone 800-832-8463
Website www.harney.com

Jacqueline's Tea Room
201 Main Street
Freeport, ME 04032
Telephone 207–865–2123
Website www.jacquelinestearoom.com

The Johnston House
7041 Crider Road
Mars, PA 16046
Telephone 724–625–2636

Mrs. Bridges Pantry
292 Rt 169
South Woodstock, CT 06267
Telephone 860–963–7040
Website www.mrsbridgespantry.com

Teaberry's
134 Main Street
Flemington, NJ 08822
908–788–1010
Website www.teaberrys.com

The Tea Leaf
487 Moody Street
Waltham, MA 02453
Telephone 781–891–1900
Website www.thetealeaf.us/

Tea and Sympathy
108 Greenwich Avenue
New York, NY 10011
Telephone 212-989-9735

T Salon
75 9th Ave
New York, NY 10011
Telephone 212-243-0432
Website www.tsalon.com

tea&tiques
408 New York Avenue
Huntington, NY 11743
Telephone 631–421-TEAS [8327]
Website www.teatiques.net/

Midwest

Lady Elegant's Tea Room & Gift Shoppe
2230 Carter Avenue
St. Paul, MN 55108
Telephone 651–645–6676
Website www.ladyelegantstea.com

Oatman House Tea Room
501 E. Main Street
Collinsville, IL 62234
Telephone 618–346–2326
Website www.oatmanhousetearoom.com/

South

De'Tours in Elizabeth City
400 W. Main Street
Elizabeth City, NC 27909
Telephone 252–435–5427
Website www.detours.embarqspace.com

English Rose Tea Room
1401 Market St.
Chattanooga, TN 37402
Telephone 423–265–5900

Gracefully Yours Tea Room & Gift Shoppe
205 W. Main Street
Vine Grove, KY 40175
Telephone 270–877–2393
Website www.gracefullyyourstearoom.com

Into My Garden Tea Room
1017 E 15th St (In the back of Nooks 'n Krannies Gift Shop)
Plano, TX 75074
Telephone 469–360–5821
Website www.intomygarden.com/

Pinkadilly Tea
303 Fauquier St
Fredericksburg, VA 22401
Telephone 540–361–1235
Website www.pinkadillytea.com/

Tea Leaves and Thyme
8990 Main Street
Woodstock, GA 30188
Telephone 770–516–2609
Website www.tealeavesandthyme.com

Tea Rose Cottage Tea Room & Boutique
1901 N. 19th. Street
Tampa, FL 33605
Telephone (813) 248–2040
Website www.tearosecottageybor.com/

This Whole House
106 East Doty Ave.
Summerville, SC 29483
Telephone 843–851–8030
www.thiswholehouse.net/

West

August Tea Room
1601 B Railroad
Livermore, CA 94550
Telephone 925–447–2822
Website www.augusttearoom.com/

Belladonna Gift Boutique and Tea Room
44054 10th Street West
Lancaster, CA 93534
Telephone 661–942–0106

English Rose
201 Easy Street #103
Carefree, AZ 85377
Telephone 480–488–4812

Lavender Tea House
16227 SW 1st Street
Sherwood, OR 97140
Telephone 503–625–4479
Website www.lavenderteahouse.com/

Queen Mary Tea Room and Restaurant
2912 Northeast 55th Street
Seattle, WA 98105
Telephone 206–527–2770
Website www.queenmarytea.com/

Tea at 1024
1024 Nuuanu Ave
Honolulu, HI 96817
Telephone 808–521–9596
Website www.teaat1024.net/

For Making Tea at Home

If you are looking for the finest tea to brew at home, I recommend Harney & Sons. They are master tea blenders who travel the world looking for the fine teas—recent trips have been to China and Japan. These exquisite teas are available in fine stores everywhere; for mail-order, please contact through Harney & Sons, P.O. Box 665, Salisbury CT 06068 and www.harney.com. You also can pay a visit to their elegant tea shop and Tasting Room in New York State (see listing under Tearooms).

Acknowledgments

Patrick—my partner in every sense of the word—for his amazing photographs that evoke so accurately the atmospheres of both the English and the Sri Lankan locations.

Belinda Boaden for her superb pattern writing skills and her friendship.

Our sample knitters—Marion Dawson, Ivy Fletcher, Frances Jago, Polly Outhwaite, Lynne Smith, Jackie White and Audrey Yates—who yet again have surpassed themselves with their extraordinary knitting talents. A special thank-you to Audrey for her beautiful embroidery.

Jules York Moore for the fabulous hair and makeup in the English chapters.

Jacquie Mei for the beautiful hair and makeup in the Sri Lankan chapters.

Anna, Deepak, Katie, Marin, Molly, Pasindu, Paul, Soraya, and Vita our wonderful models who remained cheerful throughout, however many cups of tea we got them to drink!

The Nuwara Eliya Tea Pickers who turned up to model for us impromptu!

Pasindu's Mum whose invaluable sewing skills were put to practice in Sri Lanka.

Stella Maris for helping me put together the text and her calming influence.

Gill Charlton for good advice and encouragement.

Anoma Wijewarden for providing valuable contacts in the Sri Lankan chapters.

I would like to give special thanks to the following that generously let us use their locations in England: Sue White from Cove Cottage Tea Gardens, Lucy Simpson from the Tregothnan Tea Estate, Joan Pollock from Charlotte's Tea House, Elizabeth at Smoky Joe's Truck Stop and Justin and Miki Ashton at the Lime Tree.

Nicky Grant made the beautiful cupcakes in the Green Tea chapter: www.nickygrant.com.

I would also like to give special thanks to the following that lent us locations and gave their time to make the Sri Lankan chapters possible. Jean-Marc Flambert director of the Sri Lankan Tourist Board in London. Anil Udawatte & Prasanjit Perera from the Aitken Spence Hotel Group who arranged our travel and accommodation. Roshanlal Perera and his staff at the Tea Factory Hotel in Nuwara Eliya who made us so welcome. The Somerset Tea Boutique in Nanu Oya. Chandra our wonderful driver who transported us all over Sri Lanka with such skill as well as acting as our tour guide.

Tom & Will, our sons, who have been very stoic throughout!

The team at Potter Craft—Rosy Ngo, Erica Smith, and Chi Ling Moy.

Joy Tutela, our agent extraordinaire, who has been supportive and encouraging throughout and has always believed in us.

Standard Yarn Weight System

General Guidelines for Yarn Weights

The Craft Yarn Council of America has instituted a number system for knitting and crochet yarn gauges and recommended needle and hook sizes. The information provided below is intended as a guideline, and as always, swatching is key to making sure a chosen yarn is a good match for the intended project. More information can be found at www.yarnstandards.com.

CYCA symbol	0	1	2	3	4	5
yarn weight	LACE	SUPER FINE	FINE	LIGHT	MEDIUM	BULKY
types of yarn	Fingering 10-count crochet thread	fingering, baby sock	sport baby	DK, light worsted	worsted, afgahn aran	chunky, craft rug
knit gauge* over 4" (10cm)	33–40** sts	27–32 sts	23–26 sts	21–24 sts	16–20 sts	12–15 sts
recommended needle in U.S. size range (metric size range)	U.S. 000–1 (1.5–2.25mm)	U.S. 1–3 (2.25–3.25mm)	U.S. 3–5 (3.25–3.75mm)	U.S. 5–7 (3.25–4.5mm)	U.S. 7–9 (4.5–5.5mm)	U.S. 9–11 (5.5–8mm)

*Knit gauge range in stockinette stitch.
**Fingering 10-count crochet thread. Lace-weight yarns are usually knitted or crocheted on larger needles and hooks to create lacy, openwork patterns. Accordingly, a gauge range is difficult to determine. Always follow the gauge stated in your pattern.

Index